DYSTOPIA

Steve Eddy

Series editor: Jane Sheldon

DYNAMIC LEARNING

HODDER
EDUCATION
AN HACHETTE UK COMPANY

Hachette UK's policy is to use papers that are natural, renewable and recyclable products and made from wood grown in well-managed forests and other controlled sources. The logging and manufacturing processes are expected to conform to the environmental regulations of the country of origin.

Orders: please contact Bookpoint Ltd, 130 Park Drive, Milton Park, Abingdon, Oxon OX14 4SE. Telephone: +44 (0)1235 827827. Fax: +44 (0)1235 400401. Email: education@bookpoint.co.uk Lines are open from 9 a.m. to 5 p.m., Monday to Saturday, with a 24-hour message answering service. You can also order through our website: www.hoddereducation.co.uk

ISBN: 978 1 5104 7732 2

© Steve Eddy 2020

First published in 2020 by

Hodder Education

An Hachette UK Company

Carmelite House

50 Victoria Embankment

London EC4Y 0DZ

www.hoddereducation.co.uk

Impression number   10 9 8 7 6 5 4 3 2 1

Year   2024 2023 2022 2021 2020

Cover artwork by Dylan Gibson http://www.dylangibsonillustration.co.uk

Illustrations by Integra Software Services Pvt. Ltd., Pondicherry, India

Typeset by Integra Software Services Pvt. Ltd., Pondicherry, India

Printed in Slovenia

A catalogue record for this title is available from the British Library.

Contents

The Publishers would like to thank the following for permission to reproduce copyright material.

Acknowledgements

pp. 6–7 from BRAVE NEW WORLD by Aldous Huxley Published by Vintage Reprinted by permission of The Random House Group Limited. © 2008. and © 1932, 1946 by Aldous Huxley. Reprinted by permission of Georges Borchardt, Inc., on behalf of the Aldous and Laura Huxley Trust. All rights reserved. **pp. 10–11** from NEVER LET ME GO by Kazuo Ishiguro, Faber & Faber Ltd., 2009. and © 2005 by Kazuo Ishiguro. Used by permission of Alfred A. Knopf, an imprint of the Knopf Doubleday Publishing Group, a division of Penguin Random House LLC. All rights reserved. **pp. 14–15** from THE HUNGER GAMES by Suzanne Collins. Copyright © 2008 by Suzanne Collins. Reprinted by permission of Scholastic Inc. **pp. 18–19** from ANIMAL FARM by George Orwell © 1945 by Eric Blair and renewed copyright © by the Estate of Sonia Brownell Orwell 2003. This Volume Copyright © the Estate of Sonia Brownell Orwell and Ordyr Fernando Bernardi. published by Editoria Schwarcz s.a. 2018, Houghton Milfflin Harcourt 2019, Penguin Classics 2019. and © 1946 by Houghton Mifflin Harcourt Publishing Company and renewed 1974 by Sonia Brownell Orwell. Reprinted by permission of Houghton Mifflin Harcourt Publishing Company. All rights reserved. **pp. 22–23** from 1984 by George Orwell © Eric Blair. Reprinted by kind permission of A. M. Heath & Co. Ltd. **pp. 26–27** from LORD OF THE FLIES: (PENGUIN GREAT BOOKS OF THE 20TH CENTURY) by William Golding, copyright 1954, renewed © 1982 by William Gerald Golding. Used by permission of G. P. Putnam's Sons, an imprint of Penguin Publishing Group, a division of Penguin Random House LLC. All rights reserved. and © William Golding. Reprinted by permission of Faber & Faber. **pp. 30–31** from THE HANDMAID'S TALE by Margaret Atwood © Margaret Atwood. Reprinted by permission of Penguin Random House. **pp. 34–35** from FAHRENHEIT 451 by Ray Bradbury © Ray Bradbury. Published by Faber & Faber Ltd. All rights reserved. **pp. 38–39** from 7 YEARS' SOLITARY by Edith Bone © the Estate of Edith Bone. All rights reserved. **pp. 42–43** from AN EVIL CRADLING by Brian Keenan. Reprinted by kind permission of Elaine Steel. **pp. 46–47** from FINAL DISPATCH FROM HOMS by Marie Colvin © Marie Colvin, News UK and Ireland Limited, Sunday Times, February 19, 2012. **pp. 50–51** from HIROSHIMA by John Hersey. © John Hersey. Published by Knopf Doubleday Publishing Group, a division of Penguin Random House LLC. All rights reserved. **pp. 54–55** from CHERNOBYL by Serhii Plokhy © Serhii Plokhy 2018. Published by Hachette Book Group Inc 2018, Allen Lane 2018, Penguin Books 2019. and © 2018, 2020. Reprinted by permission of Basic Books, an imprint of Hachette Book Group, Inc. **pp. 58–59** from GHOSTS OF THE TSUNAMI by Richard Lloyd Perry. Published by Vintage. Reprinted by permission of The Random House Group Limited. © 2016. **pp. 62–63** BLADE RUNNER (The Hollywood Reporter's 1982 review) by Robert Osborne. Reprinted by permission of MRC Media LLC. **pp. 66–67** 'GOING NOWHERE': THE ROAD by Deborah Ross, The Spectator, 6 January 2010. (https://www.spectator.co.uk/article/going-nowhere). **pp. 70–71** NOT MY BUSINESS by Niyi Osundare © Oluwaniyi Osundare 1990. All rights reserved. **pp. 74–75** BELFAST CONFETTI by Ciaran Carson. © Ciaran Carson. Reprinted by kind permission of the author's Estate c/o The Gallery Press, Loughcrew, Oldcastle, County Meath, Ireland from *From There to Here* (2018) and by kind permission of Wake Forest University Press, from Ciaran Carson, *The Irish For No* (1989). **pp. 78–79** OUT OF THE BLUE – 12 by Simon Armitage, from *Out of the Blue* (Enitharmon Press 2008) ISBN-13: 978-1904634584. © Simon Armitage. Reprinted by kind permission of Enitharmon Press. **pp. 82–83** AUGUST 6, 1945 by Alison Fell from *Kisses For Mayakovsky* (Virago Poets, 1984) ISBN-13: 978-0860685937. All rights reserved. **pp. 86–87** NAGASAKI: MIDORI'S ROSARY by Rowan Williams (The OtherMountain, 2014) is reprinted here by kind permission of Carcanet Press Limited, Manchester, UK. **pp. 90–91** NEIGHBOURS by Gillian Clarke © Gillian Clarke. Reprinted by kind permission of RCW Literary Agency. **pp. 94–95** THE REVIVED PIANO by Hideko Yokota, translated by Ava Yuhki. Reprinted with permission from Reverberations from Fukushima, ed. Leah Stenson and Asao Sarukawa Aroldi (Inkwater Press, 2014). **pp. 98–99** OH, HOW I WISH TO HAVE A FULL-BLOOMING CHERRY TREE by Junko Kimura. Reprinted with permission from Reverberations from Fukushima, ed. Leah Stenson and Asao Sarukawa Aroldi (Inkwater Press, 2014).

Photo credits

p. 1 t © PictureLux / The Hollywood Archive / Alamy Stock Photo; m ©kariochi - stock.adobe.com; b © jeremy sutton-hibbert / Alamy Stock Photo; **p. 3** © Erica Guilane-Nachez - stock.adobe.com; **p. 4** © Shutterstock / Everett Historical; **p. 5** © Pictorial Press Ltd / Alamy Stock Photo; **p. 6** ©fotomatrix - stock.adobe.com; **p. 8** © Antonioguillem - stock.adobe.com; **p. 9** © Africa Studio - stock.adobe.com; **p. 10** © 20th Century Fox Film Corp / Everett Collection Inc / Alamy Stock Photo; **p. 13** © 20th Century Fox Film Corp / Everett Collection Inc / Alamy Stock Photo; **p. 14** © by-studio - stock.adobe.com; **p. 16** © evbrbe - stock.adobe.com; **p. 17** © PictureLux / The Hollywood Archive / Alamy Stock Photo; **p. 18** © Everett Collection Inc / Alamy Stock Photo; **p. 20** © steturn - stock.adobe.com; **p. 21** © TNT / Everett Collection Inc / Alamy Stock Photo; **p. 22** © Prot - stock.adobe.com; **p. 24** © Mr Doomits - stock.adobe.com; **p. 25** © Umbrella-Rosenblum Films Production / Collection Christophel / Alamy Stock Photo; **p. 26** © Moviestore Collection Ltd / Alamy Stock Photo; **p. 29** © Megan - stock.adobe.com; **p. 30** © Cinecon International / Everett Collection Inc / Alamy Stock Photo; **p. 32** © Gudellaphoto - stock.adobe.com; **p. 33** © Everett Collection Inc / Alamy Stock Photo; **p. 34** © Photo 12 / Alamy Stock Photo; **p. 38** © Popperfoto via Getty Images; **p. 42** © newsfocus1 / Shutterstock; **p. 44** © Prostock-studio - stock.adobe.com; **p. 46** © Richard Young / Shutterstock; **p. 49** © Goran - stock.adobe.com; **p. 50** © agefotostock / Alamy Stock Photo; **p. 53** © Daniela - stock.adobe.com; **p. 54** Alexey Akindinov "Chernobyl. The last day of Pripyat "(Accident at the Chernobyl nuclear power plant on April 26, 1986), 120x180 cm, oil on canvas, 2013-2014; **p. 56** © Sved Oliver - stock.adobe.com; **p. 58** © kariochi - stock.adobe.com; **pp. 60–61** The Metropolitan Museum of Art, New York / H. O. Havemeyer Collection, Bequest of Mrs. H. O. Havemeyer, 1929 / https://creativecommons.org/publicdomain/zero/1.0/; **p. 62** © TCD/Prod.DB / Alamy Stock Photo; **p. 65** © Peera - stock.adobe.com; **p. 66** © Dimension Films production / Pictorial Press Ltd / Alamy Stock Photo; **p. 69** © Nejron Photo - stock.adobe.com; **p. 70** © flint01 - stock.adobe.com; **p. 71** © Ivanna Pavliuk - stock.adobe.com; **p. 74** © jeremy sutton-hibbert / Alamy Stock Photo; **p. 75** © Sergey Ryzhov - stock.adobe.com; **p. 78** © spiritofamerica - stock.adobe.com; **p. 79** © World History Archive / Alamy Stock Photo; **pp. 80–81** © Everett Collection Historical / Alamy Stock Photo; **p. 82** US National Archives and Records Administration; **p. 84** © Ben Martin / Getty Images; **p. 86** © oliver leedham / Alamy; **p. 88** © Shutterstock / Everett Historical; **p. 90** © steheap - stock.adobe.com; **p. 92** © Sid10 - stock.adobe.com; **p. 94** © Tiler84 - stock.adobe.com; **p. 96** © kelly marken - stock.adobe.com; **p. 100** © armopatt - stock.adobe.com

Introduction

What is dystopia?

In 1516, Sir Thomas More published the now-famous *Utopia*, in which he explored the idea of the perfect society where everyone could be as happy as possible - a utopia. A 'dystopia' is the opposite.

A dystopian novel is one that imagines a future world in which society has gone very wrong, so that most of the population are living in harsh conditions, often oppressed by a dictator or a powerful minority. This dystopia could be brought about by technology, politics, war or natural disaster – which are all represented in the extracts featured in this anthology.

The Industrial Revolution

The Industrial Revolution began in around 1760 and carried on well into the next century. It changed society hugely. The manufacture of iron and steel, fired by coal, led to factories that mass-produced machines and other metal goods. Cotton mills used the newly invented 'spinning jenny' to turn the cotton from Britain's foreign colonies into clothing. In one sense this was progress, and it made many manufacturers rich. However, it also meant that people who once lived in small rural communities where they knew each other and worked on the land, now increasingly moved to work in factories in rapidly growing cities like Manchester, Leeds and Liverpool.

Factory employees worked long hours performing repetitive tasks in noisy and frequently dangerous conditions. They often lived in slums in heavily polluted cities where they could not feel the same sense of belonging that they might have felt living in a village. In the Industrial Revolution, we can see how science and technological inventions might in some ways make life worse for a large part of the population. This idea has led some writers to explore how technology might create a dystopian world.

Aldous Huxley's novel *Brave New World* presents a good example of a society in which people have used science and technology to create a supposedly better world at the cost of other values, such as individual liberty and diversity. *Never Let Me Go* by Kazuo Ishiguro imagines a world in which medical science has dystopian consequences by creating human clones whose purpose in life is to 'donate' their organs to ordinary humans who need them.

In the non-fiction section, extract 13, describing the Chernobyl nuclear disaster, gives an insight into how technology intended to make human life easier can go horribly wrong.

▲ The word 'dystopia' was first used in Victorian times, but the idea was explored by writers and philosophers before that, especially in connection with the Industrial Revolution

NOW TRY THIS

Divide a large sheet of plain paper vertically into two. On one side, list ten things that you think would help to create a perfect society in any era of history or in modern times. On the opposite side, list ways in which society could go wrong and create a dystopia for most of the population.

▲ Russian propaganda poster from 1917. The text on the red banner reads 'War until Victory'

Politics and dystopia

Another element of dystopia is politics. In particular, some attempts to make society 'better' have arguably made it worse.

Revolutions

The 1789 French Revolution was led by idealists who wanted to make France a fairer place in which there were no longer huge divisions between rich and poor, and in which ordinary people had power over their own lives. Nonetheless, it led to a bloodbath in which at least 40,000 people were executed. This was followed by the dictatorship of Napoleon.

Similarly, the 1917 Russian Revolution emerged because of massive inequality in a society ruled over by the all-powerful Tsar (Emperor). The Revolution established a communist government that transferred power to the workers and redistributed wealth. It seemed to promise equality and freedom, but in fact, it led to the dictatorship of Stalin, and the murder and starvation of millions of people. Stalin is represented by a pig named Napoleon in George Orwell's novel about the Russian Revolution, *Animal Farm*, an extract from which is included in this anthology.

The abuse of power

Politics always involves power, and dystopian novels based on politics usually involve the abuse of power, whereby a powerful minority are seen to use various methods to control the majority of the population. In *Nineteen Eighty-Four*, this is done through propaganda – controlling people's minds by making them believe what the government wants them to believe – and through fear of violence or death. In *The Handmaid's Tale*, most people are forced to conform to a social role in the interests of political and social stability, but women are particularly oppressed. The oppression is supposedly justified by a warped version of Christianity.

The American novel *The Hunger Games* also imagines a future dystopian world in which members of a wealthy and powerful minority oppress the majority of the population and force them to compete with each other. The government's access to advanced technology helps them to control the population.

The characters of William Golding's novel *Lord of the Flies* are all schoolboys. Nevertheless, it raises political questions that are relevant to the adult world. Some boys choose to follow Jack, an aggressive older boy who is a good hunter. In effect, he becomes a dictator, ruling through fear and cruelty. A dwindling minority of boys still believe in civilised values and democracy, represented by a very different kind of leader, Ralph.

Terrorism and hostage-taking

Another type of dystopian activity is terrorism. In this anthology, this is represented by two poems: Ciaran Carson's 'Belfast Confetti', about the aftermath of a terrorist bomb attack in Northern Ireland, and 'Out of the Blue – 12', a poem by Simon Armitage about the plane attack on New York's World Trade Centre in 2001 (known as '9/11').

Hostage-taking can also be seen as terrorism and is used to exert pressure on more powerful enemies. This is represented by the extract from *An Evil Cradling* by Brian Keenan.

War

A final type of political dystopia is war. Wars have been taking place ever since human beings began to organise themselves into large groups. However, in modern times, the development of technology has increased our ability to inflict terrible suffering on our enemies. In this anthology, this is reflected in the non-fiction account of the nuclear bomb being dropped on Hiroshima, and in poems about this attack and the one that took place a few days later on Nagasaki.

Nature and dystopia

Although most dystopian fiction imagines a time when human beings have created their own dystopia, sometimes nature plays an important role in this. In the very bleak novel, *The Road*, we are never told what has killed off most living things apart from a relatively few surviving humans, but it could well be a natural disaster, such as a massive volcanic eruption. A review of the film adaptation is included in this anthology.

Natural disaster and technology combined in the 2011 Fukushima disaster in Japan. An underwater earthquake caused a huge tidal wave – a tsunami. This caused widespread flooding, which in turn, caused serious damage to a nuclear power plant contaminating the area with radiation. There is a first-hand account of the flood in *Ghosts of the Tsunami*, and the final two poems of this anthology's poetry section deal with the aftermath of the disaster.

▲ Dystopian novels sometimes involve a totalitarian regime and close monitoring of the population

NOW TRY THIS

In your view, what should the government of a utopian society be like? For example, how should major decisions be made? How should wealth be shared out? If there are limited resources (for example, food and fuel) should there be laws to determine how they are distributed?

Now imagine that government policy has changed to try to cope with a crisis like climate change or running out of fuel. How could this lead to a dystopian society?

NOW TRY THIS

What reasons can you think of to be optimistic about your own life, life in this country, and life worldwide? Think of at least three reasons for each category. You could think of reasons to be optimistic about human ability to tackle climate change.

WIDER READING SUGGESTIONS

If you want to read some more dystopian texts, you could try:
- Marie Lu, *Legend*
- Veronica Roth, the *Divergent* trilogy
- James Dashner, *The Maze Runner*
- Malorie Blackman, *Noughts and Crosses*.

Fiction

1 Brave New World
by Aldous Huxley

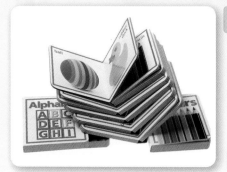

▲ The babies are conditioned to fear or dislike books

LEARNING OBJECTIVES

- To explore how the writer uses language to affect the reader's feelings
- To explore the theme of dystopian social control
- To see how the writer uses narrative techniques

CONTEXT

Aldous Huxley (1894–1963) was a novelist and philosopher who was interested in science and how it might change human life. His novel *Brave New World* was published in 1932 when the Nazis were rising to power in Germany. It explores a fictional future society in which human beings are bred to have a particular level of intelligence, among other characteristics, to make them suitable for certain jobs. There are five groups. In order of intelligence, these are Alphas, Betas, Gammas, Deltas and Epsilons. In the extract, a group of Delta babies (the second-least intelligent group) are being conditioned by the use of aversion to dislike nature and books. The Director of the baby-breeding institute demonstrates the technique to a group of students.

'Now bring in the children.'

They hurried out of the room and returned in a minute or two, each pushing a kind of tall dumb-waiter laden, on all its four wire-netted shelves, with eight-month-old babies, all exactly alike (a Bokanovsky Group, it was evident) and all (since their caste was Delta) dressed in khaki.

'Put them down on the floor.'

The infants were unloaded.

'Now turn them so that they can see the flowers and books.'

Turned, the babies at once fell silent, then began to crawl towards those clusters of sleek colours, those shapes so gay and brilliant on the white pages. As they approached, the sun came out of a momentary eclipse behind a cloud. The roses flamed up as though with a sudden passion from within; a new and profound significance seemed to suffuse the shining pages of the books. From the ranks of the crawling babies came little squeals of excitement, gurgles and twitterings of pleasure.

> The babies are brought in on wire racks, as if they are a product – like loaves of bread.

> What is the effect of the word 'unloaded'?

He is referring to the Sun coming out from behind a cloud and lighting up the books and roses.

Word choices make the babies seem innocent, enthusiastic and vulnerable.

The Director rubbed his hands. 'Excellent!' he said. 'It might almost have been done on purpose.'

The swiftest crawlers were already at their goal. Small hands reached out uncertainly, touched, grasped, unpetalling the transfigured roses, crumpling the illuminated pages of the books. The Director waited until all were happily busy. Then, 'Watch carefully,' he said. And, lifting his hand, he gave the signal.

The Head Nurse, who was standing by a switchboard at the other end of the room, pressed down a little lever.

There was a violent explosion. Shriller and ever shriller, a siren shrieked. Alarm bells maddeningly sounded.

How do you feel about the babies at this point?

The children started, screamed; their faces were distorted with terror.

'And now,' the Director shouted (for the noise was deafening), 'now we proceed to rub in the lesson with a mild electric shock.'

He waved his hand again, and the Head Nurse pressed a second lever. The screaming of the babies suddenly changed its tone. There was something desperate, almost insane, about the sharp spasmodic yelps to which they now gave utterance.

Their little bodies twitched and stiffened; their limbs moved jerkily as if to the tug of unseen wires.

'We can electrify that whole strip of floor,' bawled the Director in explanation. 'But that's enough,' he signalled to the nurse.

Huxley uses the rhetorical technique of listing three things in a row. What is the effect?

The explosions ceased, the bells stopped ringing, the shriek of the siren died down from tone to tone into silence. The stiffly twitching bodies relaxed, and what had become the sob and yelp of infant maniacs broadened out once more into a normal howl of ordinary terror.

'Offer them the flowers and the books again.'

Verb choice makes them sound almost like animals.

The nurses obeyed; but at the approach of the roses, at the mere sight of those gaily-coloured images […] the infants shrank away in horror; the volume of their howling suddenly increased.

'Observe,' said the Director triumphantly, 'observe.'

What is the Director's attitude?

This sentence is based on one from the Bible (Matthew 19:6) that is also used in a traditional wedding service: 'What God has joined together let no man put asunder.'

Books and loud noises, flowers and electric shocks – already in the infant mind these couples were compromisingly linked; and after two hundred repetitions of the same or a similar lesson would be wedded indissolubly. What man has joined, nature is powerless to put asunder.

'They'll grow up with what the psychologists used to call an "instinctive" hatred of books and flowers. Reflexes unalterably conditioned. They'll be safe from books and botany all their lives.' The Director turned to his nurses. 'Take them away again.'

▲ The babies shrank from the approach of the roses when they learned to associate them with shocks

SKILLS FOCUS

✔ Understand what is done to the babies, and why.

✔ See what impression Huxley wants to create for the reader.

LOOK CLOSER

1 How are the babies treated? Copy and complete the table below to help you explore this.

Detail	Quotation	Effect
How the babies are brought in	'laden, on all its four wire-netted shelves'	As if they are a product …
What is done to them	'There was a violent explosion. Shriller and ever shriller, a siren shrieked. Alarm bells maddeningly sounded.'	
The effect on them		
How the language makes us feel about their treatment		

2 What impression do you get of the Director? Think about:

⬡ how he gives instructions

⬡ his reactions to what happens

⬡ the way he describes the effect of the conditioning on the babies.

3 Overall, what do you think or feel about the treatment of the babies, and why?

NOW TRY THIS

1 Summarise in your own words what the Director might say if he were explaining how the aversion conditioning works and why it is necessary for the children and for the good of society.

2 Write a paragraph with one or two quotations as evidence, to show how Huxley uses language to make us feel sympathy for the babies.

FAST FINISHERS

Do you think you have been conditioned in any way to like or dislike things, for example, by your parents or teachers, or by advertising? Explain your thoughts on this question.

3 In groups of three, role-play a TV discussion with someone who is in favour of breeding and conditioning babies for roles in society and someone who opposes this. The third person should play the part of the 'chair', whose role it is to raise questions and make sure each person has a chance to speak and deal with their opponent's arguments.

❓ PRACTICE QUESTION

Choose **four** statements below which are **true**.

✪ Copy out the ones that you think are true.

✪ Choose a maximum of four true statements.   [4 marks]

A The children are treated kindly.   ☐

B The children are all very similar.   ☐

C The Director hates alarming the babies.   ☐

D The nurse obeys the Director.   ☐

E The conditioning takes place in a windowless room.   ☐

F The Director is pleased with his demonstration.   ☐

G The babies are given a severe electric shock.   ☐

H The conditioning process is very noisy.   ☐

◀ Why do you think all the babies look alike in the extract?

2 Never Let Me Go

by Kazuo Ishiguro

▲ Kathy (played by Carey Mulligan) in the 2010 film adaptation

LEARNING OBJECTIVES

- To learn about characterisation in a first-person narrative
- To explore the theme of duty
- To see how texts fit into their cultural and historical settings

CONTEXT

Ishiguro was born in 1954 in Nagasaki, Japan – a city that had an atomic bomb dropped on it in 1945. He moved to Britain at the age of five. *Never Let Me Go* is a first-person narrative novel which imagines a world in which some people are genetically copied (cloned). Clones are raised to be organ donors (for example, of their lungs or kidneys). Some of them, like Kathy, the narrator, act as carers for other clones until they are told they must start to make their own organ 'donations'.

Cloned children brought up in a boarding school called Hailsham have a better early life than others. Some of the teachers there campaign to prove that clones are really human. Eventually, all clones make their fourth 'donation' (probably the heart) and 'complete' (die).

> She has no parents to inherit a surname from, so the 'H' could stand for Hailsham.

> The novel never reveals who 'they' are.

My name is Kathy H. I'm thirty-one years old, and I've been a carer now for over eleven years. That sounds long enough, I know, but actually they want me to go on for another eight months, until the end of this year. That'll make it almost exactly twelve years. Now I know my being a carer so long isn't necessarily because they think I'm fantastic at what I do. There are some really good carers who've been told to stop after just two or three years. And I can think of one carer at least who went on for all of fourteen years despite being a complete waste of space. So I'm not trying to boast. But then I do know for a fact they've been pleased with my work, and by and large, I have too. My donors have always tended to do much better than expected. Their recovery times have been impressive, and hardly any of them have been classified as 'agitated', even before fourth donation. Okay, maybe I *am* boasting now.

> This makes it seem quite random, but Kathy just seems to accept that it's not up to her to question the decision-makers.

But it means a lot to me, being able to do my work well, especially that bit about my donors staying 'calm'. I've developed a kind of instinct around donors. I know when to hang around and comfort them, when to leave them to themselves; when to listen to everything they have to say, and when just to shrug and tell them to snap out of it.

Anyway, I'm not making any big claims for myself. I know carers, working now, who are just as good and don't get half the credit. If you're one of them, I can understand how you might get resentful – about my bedsit, my car, above all, the way I get to pick and choose who I look after. And I'm a Hailsham student – which is enough by itself sometimes to get people's backs up. Kathy H., they say, she gets to pick and choose, and she always chooses her own kind: people from Hailsham, or one of the other privileged estates. No wonder she has a great record. I've heard it said enough, so I'm sure you've heard it plenty more, and maybe there's something in it. But I'm not the first to be allowed to pick and choose, and I doubt if I'll be the last. And anyway, I've done my share of looking after donors brought up in every kind of place. By the time I finish, remember, I'll have done twelve years of this, and it's only for the last six they've let me choose.

And why shouldn't they? Carers aren't machines. You try and do your best for every donor, but in the end, it wears you down. You don't have unlimited patience and energy. So when you get a chance to choose, of course, you choose your own kind. That's natural. There's no way I could have gone on for as long as I have if I'd stopped feeling for my donors every step of the way. And anyway, if I'd never started choosing, how would I ever have got close again to Ruth and Tommy after all those years?

But these days, of course, there are fewer and fewer donors left who I remember, and so in practice, I haven't been choosing that much. As I say, the work gets a lot harder when you don't have that deeper link with the donor, and though I'll miss being a carer, it feels just about right to be finishing at last come the end of the year.

What impression do you get of Kathy from her language and what she says about herself?

What is the effect of how Kathy addresses the reader here? And what impression do you get of a clone's life from the things she thinks other carers might be jealous of?

She defends herself against the criticisms she imagines you, the reader, might make, thus involving the reader in the narrative.

This is the first mention of Kathy's old childhood friends. She seems to assume the reader knows who they are.

Gradually, all the people she knew are 'completing' (dying). She seems to accept this uncomplainingly.

LOOK CLOSER

1 What key information do we learn about Kathy and her life? Consider:
- ✪ what she does
- ✪ what benefits she has and her attitude towards these
- ✪ what she expects people to think of her
- ✪ what she thinks of herself.

2 What impression of Kathy do you get from the way she addresses the reader? Copy and complete the table below, and add at least one more quotation.

Quotation	What it says about her
'I do know for a fact they've been pleased with my work, and by and large, I have too.'	She takes satisfaction in knowing that …
'I know carers, working now, who are just as good and don't get half the credit.'	
'Okay, maybe I *am* boasting now.'	
'And why shouldn't they? Carers aren't machines.'	

3 What is Kathy's attitude towards finishing being a carer, and how do you feel about this? Consider:
- ✪ what will happen to her when she finishes
- ✪ what you might feel if you were her.

4 Find three examples of Kathy's language being casual and conversational. Consider:
- ✪ her word choices
- ✪ types of sentence
- ✪ what she might say if she were being more formal.

NOW TRY THIS

1. Write two paragraphs explaining at least two important things that you learn about Kathy's life and her attitude towards it here.

2. Write an alternative opening to the novel using third-person narrative to convey some of the information that the real opening provides. You could begin with something like this: 'Kathy H climbed into her car and placed on the passenger seat a folder of notes on the next donor she was about to visit …'

3. Write what you might say to Kathy, or ask her, if you had the opportunity to meet her and question her acceptance of her fate as an involuntary organ 'donor'. Start by asking yourself how you might feel if you had to look after people having to 'donate' their organs, then die, and eventually do the same yourself.

FAST FINISHERS

Write the opening to an episode in which Kathy, as a carer, has her first meeting with a donor.

3. Discuss what moral or ethical issues you think this novel would explore, based on the *Context* section above and the extract itself.

❓ PRACTICE QUESTION

What do you learn about the character of Kathy in this extract? Use evidence from the text to back up your findings. Consider:

- ✪ how she seems to accept her role
- ✪ how she addresses the reader
- ✪ what she prides herself on.   [8 marks]

◀ Ella Purnell and Izzy Meikle-Small as Ruth and Kathy as children in the 2010 film adaptation of *Never Let Me Go*

3 The Hunger Games

by Suzanne Collins

▲ A wasp nest

LEARNING OBJECTIVES

- ✪ To analyse the character of Katniss
- ✪ To explore the theme of power
- ✪ To explore narrative technique

CONTEXT

The extract is from a novel set in a dystopian future version of the United States called Panem; the majority of the population have in the past rebelled unsuccessfully against the central government, based in a distant city called the Capitol. The government have destroyed the district that led the rebellion – District 13.

As an ongoing punishment for this rebellion, and as a reminder of the power of the elite, the remaining twelve districts are forced to compete with each other every year in the Hunger Games. Each district has to provide two 'tributes', one male and one female, aged 12–18. All the tributes have to fight each other to the death in a huge outdoor arena over several weeks. This arena is full of hidden cameras so that the whole event can be televised. The Capitol also have the power to introduce new perils to the arena to make the 'games' more exciting for viewers in the Capitol.

The novel is narrated by the main character, Katniss Everdeen. At the start of the extract, she has climbed a tree to escape other tributes who are pursuing her. They are still asleep at the bottom of the tree.

How is this sentence more effective than just saying 'it is dawn'?

Rosy streaks are breaking through in the east. I can't afford to wait any longer. Compared to the agony of last night's climb, this one is a cinch. At the tree limb that holds the nest, I position the knife in the groove and I'm about to draw the teeth across the wood when I see something moving. There, on the nest. The bright gold gleam of a **tracker jacker** lazily making its way across the papery grey surface. No question, it's acting a little subdued, but the wasp is up and moving and

Earlier, Katniss was burned by a fireball attack staged by the games' controllers, but then she won enough sympathy to be awarded some healing ointment which now makes climbing (to reach a wasp nest) much less painful. The Capitol has the power to make things easier as well as harder for her.

that means the others will be out soon as well. Sweat breaks out on the palms of my hands, beading up through the ointment, and I do my best to pat them dry on my shirt. If I don't get through this branch in a matter of seconds, the entire swarm could emerge and attack me.

The novel is written in the present tense. How does it work especially well here to give a sense of what is at stake?

How does the author create a sense of drama and suspense here?

There's no sense in putting it off. I take a deep breath, grip the knife handle and bear down as hard as I can. Back, forth, back, forth! The tracker jackers begin to buzz and I hear them coming out. Back, forth, back, forth! A stabbing pain shoots through my knee and I know one has found me and the others will be honing in. Back, forth, back, forth. And just as the knife cuts through, I shove the end of the branch as far away from me as I can. It crashes down through the lower branches, snagging temporarily on a few but then twisting free until it smashes with a thud on the ground. The nest bursts open like an egg, and a furious swarm of tracker jackers takes to the air.

I feel a second sting on the cheek, a third on my neck, and their venom almost immediately makes me woozy. I cling to the tree with one arm while I rip the barbed stingers out of my flesh. Fortunately, only these three tracker jackers had identified me before the nest went down. The rest of the insects have targeted their enemies on the ground.

How do the details and language (for example, 'rip the barbed stingers') make the passage come alive and make us sympathise with Katniss?

This topic sentence briefly tells the reader what the rest of the paragraph will describe. So, what do you think 'mayhem' means?

It's mayhem. The Careers have woken to a full-scale tracker-jacker attack. Peeta and a few others have the sense to drop everything and bolt. I can hear cries of 'To the lake! To the lake!' and know they hope to evade the wasps by taking to the water. It must be close if they think they can outdistance the furious insects. Glimmer and another girl, the one from District 4, are not so lucky. They receive multiple stings before they're even out of my view. Glimmer appears to go completely mad, shrieking and trying to bat the wasps off with her bow, which is pointless. She calls to the others for help but, of course, no one returns. The girl from District 4 staggers out of sight, although I wouldn't bet on her making it to the lake. I watch Glimmer fall, twitch hysterically around on the ground for a few minutes, and then go still.

What does this tell us about the tributes' attitude towards each other?

▲ Tracker jackers are genetically engineered wasps that have been created by the Capitol. Unlike natural wasps, once they make a person their target, they will follow them far away from their nest

GLOSSARY

tracker jacker: genetically mutated wasp with a potentially lethal sting; they 'track' their target relentlessly

Career: young person specially trained to compete in the Hunger Games

Peeta: the male tribute from the same district as Katniss

SKILLS FOCUS

✔ Understand the character of Katniss.

✔ Analyse how the author makes the narrative compelling.

LOOK CLOSER

1. What is Katniss aiming to do in this passage? Consider:
   - why she climbs higher in the tree
   - what she does with her knife
   - what happens to the tributes down below.

2. What do you learn about the character and abilities of Katniss? Consider:
   - her plan
   - what she has to do to achieve it
   - how she copes with what happens.

3. How does the author make this narrative exciting? Copy and complete the table below to help you consider this. Add at least one further quotation or detail.

Quotation/Detail	Effect
'I can't afford to wait any longer.'	This shows how urgent her situation is.
'Sweat breaks out on the palms of my hands'	This physical detail shows …
'There's no sense in putting it off. I take a deep breath …'	

NOW TRY THIS

1 Imagine you're a journalist in the Capitol presenting the Hunger Games to viewers. Write what you might say about the wasp episode to make viewers interested in Katniss and want to support her.

2 Explain in three paragraphs how this whole episode explores the theme of power. Consider:

- ✿ the situation at the start of the extract
- ✿ how Katniss changes it
- ✿ how the episode shows the power of the Capitol.

FAST FINISHERS

Choose a sentence that you think helps to make the passage exciting. Explain how it does this. Then make up a new sentence of your own that adds to the sense of drama.

3 Discuss how you think you would cope in a 'dog-eat-dog' situation like the one Katniss is in. Consider:

- ✿ Would you be prepared to attack others to save yourself?
- ✿ Would you attack others to save your friends or family?
- ✿ How would you keep up your spirits and keep going?

❓ PRACTICE QUESTION

What do you learn about the Hunger Games in this scene? Support your ideas with evidence from the text. Consider:

- ✿ how the tributes treat each other
- ✿ what they have to cope with
- ✿ the aim of the games.   [8 marks]

◀ Jennifer Lawrence as Katniss Everdeen in the 2012 film adaptation of The Hunger Games

4 Animal Farm
by George Orwell

▲ A 1917 Russian revolutionary propaganda poster. *Animal Farm* is an allegory based on the Russian Revolution

LEARNING OBJECTIVES

- To understand hidden and implied meanings
- To learn about the characterisation of Snowball, Napoleon and the dogs
- To understand satirical allegory in its historical setting

CONTEXT

Animal Farm was published in 1945, at the end of the Second World War. It tells the story of a farm in England where the animals rebel against the farmer and establish a new rule of equality where no animal is exploited. However, the pigs gradually gain power and form a ruling elite headed by the chief pig, Napoleon.

Orwell called the book 'a fairy story', ironically pretending that it had no deeper meaning. In fact, it is an allegory – a story with a hidden meaning and moral – based on the Russian Revolution of 1917 and the rise to power of Stalin, who became a dictator. The novel is also a satire – a work that uses humour to mock and criticise a system or individuals.

In the extract, the character of Napoleon is based on Stalin, and Snowball on another leading communist, Trotsky, whom Stalin had murdered. The dogs represent the secret police who enforced communist rule. Mr Jones, the farmer, represents the Tsar, who was the supreme leader of pre-Revolution Russia. Major, who dies at the start of the novel, represents Karl Marx, the philosopher who developed the theory of communist revolution.

The animals are discussing whether to pursue Snowball's plan to build a windmill to grind their corn and generate electricity.

> How do verbs and adjectives create an impression of Snowball here and in the rest of the paragraph?

At this Snowball sprang to his feet, and shouting down the sheep, who had begun bleating again, broke into a passionate appeal in favour of the windmill. Until now the animals had been about equally divided in their sympathies, but in a moment Snowball's **eloquence** had carried them away. In glowing sentences he painted a picture of Animal Farm as it might be when **sordid** labour was lifted from the animals' backs. His imagination had now run far beyond **chaff**-cutters and **turnip**-slicers.

Electricity, he said, could operate **threshing** machines, ploughs, **harrows**, rollers, and reapers and binders, besides supplying every **stall** with its own electric light, hot and cold water, and an electric heater. By the time he had finished speaking, there was no doubt as to which way the vote would go. But just at this moment Napoleon stood up and, casting a peculiar sidelong look at Snowball, uttered a high-pitched whimper of a kind no one had ever heard him utter before.

At this there was a terrible baying sound outside, and nine enormous dogs wearing brass-studded collars came bounding into the barn. They dashed straight for Snowball, who only sprang from his place just in time to escape their snapping jaws. In a moment he was out of the door and they were after him. Too amazed and frightened to speak, all the animals crowded through the door to watch the chase. Snowball was racing across the long pasture that led to the road. He was running as only a pig can run, but the dogs were close on his heels. Suddenly he slipped and it seemed certain that they had him. Then he was up again, running faster than ever, then the dogs were gaining on him again. One of them all but closed his jaws on Snowball's tail, but Snowball whisked it free just in time. Then he put on an extra spurt and, with a few inches to spare, slipped through a hole in the hedge and was seen no more.

Silent and terrified, the animals crept back into the barn. In a moment the dogs came bounding back. At first no one had been able to imagine where these creatures came from, but the problem was soon solved: they were the puppies whom Napoleon had taken away from their mothers and reared privately. Though not yet full-grown, they were huge dogs, and as fierce-looking as wolves. They kept close to Napoleon. It was noticed that they wagged their tails to him in the same way as the other dogs had been used to do to Mr Jones.

Napoleon, with the dogs following him, now mounted on to the raised portion of the floor where Major had previously stood to deliver his speech. He announced that from now on the Sunday-morning Meetings would come to an end. They were unnecessary, he said, and wasted time. In future all questions relating to the working of the farm would be settled by a special committee of pigs, presided over by himself. These would meet in private and afterwards communicate their decisions to the others. The animals would still assemble on Sunday mornings to salute the flag, sing **'Beasts of England'**, and receive their orders for the week; but there would be no more debates.

Look at how Orwell uses verbs to make this development sound dramatic.

This phrase makes it sound as if, once the animals know where the dogs come from, they are no longer a problem.

Orwell often uses the passive voice in this way, so that the one doing the 'noticing' remains anonymous.

The democracy has become a dictatorship, with some power given by Napoleon to a small elite.

Napoleon does not want debates on farm policy. He just wants to give orders and be obeyed.

The dogs used to want to please Mr Jones (who represents the Tsar), so their similar behaviour towards Napoleon (Stalin) suggests that he is like a new Tsar – so the Revolution has achieved nothing!

He stands where Major (who represents Marx) once stood. What does this suggest about how he sees himself and how he wants to be seen by the other animals?

They will 'receive their orders' from the pigs.

GLOSSARY

eloquence: elegant, well-expressed and persuasive language

sordid: disgusting, demeaning, lowly

chaff: outer husks of wheat – what is left after the grain has been removed

turnip: a root vegetable often fed to cattle

threshing: the process of removing grain from wheat husks

harrows: metal tools dragged over the ground after ploughing to prepare it for planting

stall: a 'room' where animals sleep

Beasts of England: a stirring revolutionary song, like the socialist song 'The Red Flag'

▲ Snowball wants to build a windmill to grind corn and generate electricity

SKILLS FOCUS

✔ Understand the characterisation of Snowball, Napoleon and the dogs.

✔ Understand satirical allegory.

LOOK CLOSER

1 What impression do you get of Snowball? Consider:
   - the language Orwell uses to describe him (especially adjectives and verbs)
   - what he promises to the animals
   - how his status changes when pursued by the dogs.

2 What impression do you get of Napoleon? Consider:
   - his training of the dogs
   - his exercise of power
   - his new rules.

3 How are the dogs presented? Consider:
   - the noise they make
   - their appearance
   - their actions
   - their obedience.

4 What political process is Orwell allegorically representing in this extract? Re-read the *Context* section above if you need to.

NOW TRY THIS

1 Imagine that you are an intelligent animal (but not a pig or dog) who is present at this event. Describe your experience and what you felt about it then, and now.

2 Imagine that, years later, Napoleon (representing Stalin) writes his autobiography. Write his account of this episode, showing himself in a positive way and Snowball in a negative way. Here are some possible sentence starters:

✪ 'I knew that the simple animals couldn't really think for themselves. They needed a strong leader …'

✪ 'I needed the dogs to bring out the best in the other animals …'

✪ 'The traitor, Snowball, was always self-obsessed …'

FAST FINISHERS

Make up a newspaper headline and opening paragraph for a pro-Napoleon news feature describing this event.

3 In small groups, role-play the first meeting of the 'special committee of pigs', headed by Napoleon. Discuss what you have achieved so far, and how you should now develop the farm and consolidate (build on) your authority.

❓ PRACTICE QUESTION

How does Orwell engage the reader in what happens in this episode?
Consider:

✪ how he surprises the reader

✪ how he uses language

✪ how he makes the importance of this episode clear.   [8 marks]

◀ Why do you think Orwell chose pigs to represent the new elite?

5 Nineteen Eighty-Four

by George Orwell

▲ Rats are Winston's greatest fear

CONTEXT

The novel was published in 1949 and is set 35 years into the future. In *Nineteen Eighty-Four*, Orwell imagines a world divided into three huge states that are always at war with one another. Democracy does not exist. Britain, now called Airstrip One, is part of a superstate, Oceania, ruled by an authoritarian government headed by a dictator known only as Big Brother. The government makes widespread use of propaganda, rewrites history, and forces people to take part in events such as Hate Week, when they are encouraged to whip up their feelings of hatred for an enemy of the state. The Thought Police constantly monitor everyone's behaviour.

In this extract, near the end of the novel, the main character, Winston, is paying the price for rebelling in relatively small ways against the government. One of his crimes is having an affair with a woman called Julia. He has been taken to Room 101 by O'Brien, a government official, for interrogation and re-education in obedience to the state. Prisoners taken there are faced with whatever is their worst nightmare.

Fear has made Winston 'disassociate' – distancing himself mentally from his situation.

····►

There was an outburst of squeals from the cage. It seemed to reach Winston from far away. The rats were fighting; they were trying to get at each other through the partition. He heard also a deep groan of despair. That, too, seemed to come from outside himself.

O'Brien picked up the cage, and, as he did so, pressed something in it. There was a sharp click. Winston made a frantic effort to tear himself loose from the chair. It was hopeless; every part of him, even his head, was held immovably. O'Brien moved the cage nearer. It was less than a metre from Winston's face.

Why do you think O'Brien explains the process to Winston rather than just releasing the rats? What is the effect on Winston, and on the reader?

'I have pressed the first lever,' said O'Brien. 'You understand the construction of this cage. The mask will fit over your head, leaving no exit. When I press this other lever, the door of the cage will slide up. These starving brutes will shoot out of it like bullets. Have you ever seen a rat leap through the air? They will leap on to your face and bore straight into it. Sometimes they attack the eyes first. Sometimes they burrow through the cheeks and devour the tongue.'

The cage was nearer; it was closing in. Winston heard a succession of shrill cries which appeared to be occurring in the air above his head. But he fought furiously against his panic. To think, to think, even with a split second left – to think was the only hope. Suddenly the foul musty odour of the brutes struck his nostrils. There was a violent convulsion of nausea inside him, and he almost lost consciousness. Everything had gone black. For an instant he was insane, a screaming animal. Yet he came out of the blackness clutching an idea. There was one and only one way to save himself. He must interpose another human being, the body of another human being, between himself and the rats.

Why does Winston try to think? For example, is he trying to think of a way to escape?

He begins to consider betrayal.

The circle of the mask was large enough now to shut out the vision of anything else. The wire door was a couple of hand-spans from his face. The rats knew what was coming now. One of them was leaping up and down, the other, an old scaly grandfather of the sewers, stood up, with his pink hands against the bars, and fiercely sniffed the air. Winston could see the whiskers and the yellow teeth. Again the black panic took hold of him. He was blind, helpless, mindless.

Look at how Orwell uses details and language ('leaping … scaly … fiercely') to create a vivid impression of the rats.

O'Brien seems entirely calm and matter-of-fact about the terrible torture he inflicts.

'It was a common punishment in Imperial China,' said O'Brien as didactically as ever.

The mask was closing on his face. The wire brushed his cheek. And then – no, it was not relief, only hope, a tiny fragment of hope. Too late, perhaps too late. But he had suddenly understood that in the whole world there was just one person to whom he could transfer his punishment – one body that he could thrust between himself and the rats. And he was shouting frantically, over and over.

'Do it to Julia! Do it to Julia! Not me! Julia! I don't care what you do to her. Tear her face off, strip her to the bones. Not me! Julia! Not me!'

Just after this, O'Brien halts the punishment: he keeps the rats in their cage. He knows that Winston's loyalty is now entirely to the state, because he is prepared to betray Julia completely.

▲ Prisoners face their worst nightmare in room 101

GLOSSARY

didactically: in a way aimed at imparting knowledge

SKILLS FOCUS

✔ Understand Winston's state of mind.

✔ Explore Orwell's narrative technique.

LOOK CLOSER

1. What do we learn about Winston's state of mind and how it develops during the extract? Consider:
   - how he distances himself from what is happening
   - his panic and efforts to make himself think
   - his realisation and why it is important.

2. How does Orwell create dramatic tension in the scene? Copy and complete the table below to help you explore this, and add at least one more quotation.

Quotation	What it shows
'Winston made a frantic effort to tear himself loose from the chair.'	Winston is desperate to escape but is trapped helplessly in the chair, at O'Brien's mercy.
'It was less than a metre from Winston's face. [...] The cage was nearer; it was closing in.'	Orwell describes the cage as gradually moving nearer …
'One of them was leaping up and down'	

3. What impression do you get of O'Brien's character? Consider:
   - what he tells Winston
   - how he speaks
   - what he is doing.

4. What is the impact on the reader of Winston finally giving in under pressure? Consider:
   - what he says
   - what this suggests about how Room 101 has affected him
   - what you think of him as the 'hero' of the novel.

NOW TRY THIS

1. Write what O'Brien might say to a group of students that he was training in interrogation and the use of Room 101. Consider what he might say about:
   - the purpose of Room 101
   - his techniques
   - his justification for using such techniques
   - some examples of people he has 're-educated'.

2. Write your own scene in which someone like Winston is faced with something they fear in Room 101. It can be anything you like; it does not have to be something that would frighten everyone.

FAST FINISHERS

Imagine you are in O'Brien's position. Write your report on a successful session – either the one with Winston, or the one you made up.

3. In *Nineteen Eighty-Four*, the government wants everyone to be completely loyal to the state, not to anything or anyone else. Discuss your views on loyalty. Who or what deserves your loyalty? Do you feel you should be loyal to your school, to your country, or to what you believe in?

❓ PRACTICE QUESTION

How does Orwell make the reader feel what Winston is going through in this extract? Consider:

- his situation and what details reveal it
- how Orwell creates a sense of the desperation and urgency that Winston must feel
- how Orwell makes us imagine the rats and what will happen to Winston. [8 marks]

◀ In 1984, Orwell's novel was adapted into a film. Looking at this still from the film, what do you think inspired Orwell to write about an authoritarian government?

6 Lord of the Flies

by William Golding

▲ Piggy with the conch, with Ralph and Jack confronting each other, in the 1990 film adaptation of Golding's novel

LEARNING OBJECTIVES

⊙ To learn how Golding explores the theme of civilisation versus savagery

⊙ To explore the characters of Ralph and Piggy

⊙ To see how texts fit into their cultural and historical settings

CONTEXT

Lord of the Flies is set on a tropical island where a number of boys are marooned after their plane is shot down during a war. They live on fruit and meat from wild pigs that they hunt. They have meetings where they try to decide on rules for living harmoniously on the island, and how to get rescued. One boy, Ralph, is elected leader, and it is agreed that in their meetings the boy holding the conch – a large seashell – is the one allowed to speak at that point. The conch is also blown like a trumpet to gather everyone together. It therefore becomes a symbol of civilised values and democracy. It is also agreed that a boy named Jack will lead 'the hunters'.

Early in the novel, the boys agree to keep a fire burning on a mountain to attract the attention of passing ships so that they have a chance of rescue. However, they let the fire go out, so at least one ship passes without them being spotted.

The extract is taken from near the end of the novel, when civilised values have mostly broken down. Jack has become a rival leader to Ralph, and has led his followers to live separately at one end of the island. Ralph and the overweight, short-sighted boy nick-named Piggy remain living on the beach with a few others. Jack and his hunters have just raided Ralph and Piggy's hut and stolen Piggy's glasses to use to start a fire.

Ralph and Piggy are loyal to the world of 'grown-ups', who represent civilisation (although they start wars!), so they want to be rescued. But this question also relates to human beings in general.

'I just take the conch to say this. I can't see no more and I got to get my glasses back. Awful things has been done on this island. I voted for you for chief. He's the only one who ever got anything done. So now you speak, Ralph, and tell us what. Or else –'

Piggy broke off, snivelling. Ralph took back the conch as he sat down.

'Just an ordinary fire. You'd think we could do that, wouldn't you? Just a smoke signal so we can be rescued. Are we savages or what? Only now there's no signal going up. Ships may be passing. Do you remember how he went hunting and the fire went

Piggy refers to the night when the boys beat one boy, Simon, to death, thinking he was 'the Beast' – an imagined creature who seems to embody all their fears.

26

Ralph cannot bear to spell out the fact that they all killed Simon. He blames Jack. Is it normal human behaviour to blame others?

What is he trying to achieve? What do you think of his idea?

Piggy worries about what adults will think if they are rescued. But he is also brave enough to admit that Simon was murdered.

Piggy believes in right and wrong. He thinks Jack will have to admit that he behaved wrongly. How much chance do you think Piggy has of persuading Jack?

Ralph's weakness as a leader is that he cannot think through a problem. It is as if a curtain comes down so he loses sight of his train of thought.

He has been hurt in Jack's attack. His cheek is swollen, so he has to pull it down to see properly.

Remember: the conch symbolises civilised values, so Golding is suggesting that these values are beautiful but fragile.

out and a ship passed by? And they all think he's best as chief. Then there was, there was … that's his fault, too. If it hadn't been for him it would never have happened. Now Piggy can't see, and they came, stealing –' Ralph's voice ran up '– at night, in darkness, and stole our fire. They stole it. We'd have given them fire if they'd asked. But they stole it and the signal's out and we can't ever be rescued. Don't you see what I mean? We'd have given them fire for themselves only they stole it. I –' He paused lamely as the curtain flickered in his brain. Piggy held out his hands for the conch.

'What you goin' to do, Ralph? This is jus' talk without deciding. I want my glasses.'

'I'm trying to think. Supposing we go, looking like we used to, washed and hair brushed – after all we aren't savages really and being rescued isn't a game –'

He opened the flap of his cheek and looked at the twins.

'We could smarten up a bit and then go –'

'We ought to take spears,' said Sam. 'Even Piggy.'

'– because we may need them.'

'You haven't got the conch!'

Piggy held up the shell.

'You can take spears if you want but I shan't. What's the good? I'll have to be led like a dog, anyhow. Yes, laugh. Go on, laugh. There's them on this island as would laugh at anything. And what happened? What's grown-ups goin' to think? Young Simon was murdered. And there was that other kid what had a mark on his face. Who's seen him since we first come here?'

'Piggy! Stop a minute!'

'I got the conch. I'm going to that Jack Merridew an' tell him, I am.'

'You'll get hurt.'

'What can he do more than he has? I'll tell him what's what. You let me carry the conch, Ralph. I'll show him the one thing he hasn't got.'

Piggy paused for a moment and peered round at the dim figures. The shape of the old assembly, trodden in the grass, listened to him.

'I'm going to him with this conch in my hands. I'm going to hold it out. Look, I'm goin' to say, you're stronger than I am and you haven't got asthma. You can see, I'm goin' to say, and with both eyes. But I don't ask for my glasses back, not as a favour. I don't ask you to be a sport, I'll say, not because you're strong, but because what's right's right. Give me my glasses, I'm going to say – you got to!'

Piggy ended, flushed and trembling. He pushed the conch quickly into Ralph's hands as though in a hurry to be rid of it and wiped the tears from his eyes. The green light was gentle about them and the conch lay at Ralph's feet, fragile and white.

SKILLS FOCUS

✔ Explore the theme of civilisation versus savagery.
✔ Understand the characters of Ralph and Piggy.

LOOK CLOSER

1 What impression do you get of Piggy? Copy and complete the table below to explore this.

Quotation	What it shows
'Awful things has been done on this island.'	Piggy strongly disapproves of the breakdown of civilised values.
'What you goin' to do, Ralph? This is jus' talk without deciding.'	Piggy is not a natural leader but …
'Young Simon was murdered.'	
'Give me my glasses, I'm going to say – you got to!'	

2 What impression do you get of Ralph as a leader? Consider:
   ☢ how he speaks
   ☢ his ability to think
   ☢ his values.

3 How does Golding use the conch as a symbol? Consider:
   ☢ how it is used
   ☢ how Golding describes it
   ☢ how Piggy intends to use it.

4 Make a table like the one below to show Piggy's uses of non-standard English. In the right-hand column, suggest what a more standard version would be.

Example	Standard version
'I can't see no more.'	'I can't see anymore.'
'I got to.'	

NOW TRY THIS

1 Make a list clearly summarising the points that Ralph tries to make.

2 Write a paragraph explaining Piggy's argument for Jack returning his glasses. Bear in mind what Piggy implies (for example, by carrying the conch – a symbol of civilised values) as well as what he explicitly says.

3 Imagine you are Jack. Write the short speech you might make to your followers, telling them how you are going to attack Ralph and steal Piggy's glasses, and why this is justified.

FAST FINISHERS

Make your own bullet-point list of rules for how you think people should treat each other in society.

4 Discuss what you understand by:
- ✪ civilisation
- ✪ human rights.

Try to reach a definition of each.

❓ PRACTICE QUESTION

How does Golding explore the theme of civilisation versus savagery in this extract? Write about:

- ✪ what has happened on the island – Jack breaking away with his 'hunters', and one boy getting killed
- ✪ Ralph's complaints
- ✪ Piggy's ideas about how they should behave, and what is right
- ✪ what makes boys like Jack reject civilised values.   [8 marks]

◀ Why do you think Golding chose a conch as the symbol of civilisation?

7 The Handmaid's Tale
by Margaret Atwood

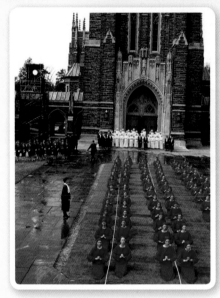

▲ Handmaids from the 1990 film adaptation

LEARNING OBJECTIVES

⊙ To learn how Atwood explores the theme of the individual and society

⊙ To explore how character is expressed through narrative

⊙ To see how texts fit into their cultural and historical settings

CONTEXT

The novel is set in a future America, called Gilead, ruled by a one-party government. Gilead is very male-dominated, and individual liberties are restricted by laws enforced by harsh penalties. Its values are based on the Old Testament of the Bible.

Fertility rates have fallen dramatically: few couples can have babies. Fertile women are forced to become 'Handmaids' to powerful men, attempting to bear children for them and their wives. They are indoctrinated by older women known as 'Aunts' to believe that being Handmaids is an honour, and that women should serve men. Handmaids must wear long red dresses with white headdresses that partly hide their faces. Male 'Guardians' control and protect them.

In the extract, the narrator, Offred, meets another Handmaid, Ofglen. They take their names from their 'Commanders': Fred and Glen. They are shopping partners.

This metaphor could suggest that the Handmaids are encouraged to have 'tunnel vision', only understanding the world in an orthodox way.

They are expected to report if the other Handmaid does or says anything rebellious.

A shape, red with white wings around the face, a shape like mine, a nondescript woman in red carrying a basket, comes along the brick sidewalk towards me. She reaches me and we peer at each other's faces, looking down the white tunnels of cloth that enclose us. She is the right one.

'Blessed be the fruit,' she says to me, the accepted greeting among us.

'May the Lord open,' I answer, the accepted response. We turn and walk together past the large houses, towards the central part of town. We aren't allowed to go there except in twos. This is supposed to be for our protection, though the notion is absurd: we are well protected already. The truth is that she is my spy, as I am hers. If either of us slips through the net because of something that happens on one of our daily walks, the other will be accountable.

This woman has been my partner for two weeks. I don't know what happened to the one before. On a certain day she simply wasn't

---

The standard greeting and response among Handmaids are taken from the Bible and are supposed to help them become pregnant. Both phrases are associated in the Bible with women unexpectedly becoming pregnant.

---

there anymore, and this one was there in her place. It isn't the sort of thing you ask questions about, because the answers are not usually answers you want to know. Anyway there wouldn't be an answer.

What kind of answer might there be?

This one is a little plumper than I am. Her eyes are brown. Her name is Ofglen, and that's about all I know about her. She walks **demurely**, head down, red-gloved hands clasped in front, with short little steps like a trained pig's on its hind legs. During these walks she has never said anything that was not strictly **orthodox**, but then, neither have I. She may be a real believer, a Handmaid in more than name. I can't take the risk.

This simile makes Ofglen sound ridiculous. Later in the novel, Offred and Ofglen become friends.

'The war is going well, I hear,' she says.

'Praise be,' I reply.

They are supposed to express gratitude to God for anything that is good for the government.

'We've been sent good weather.'

'Which I receive with joy.'

'They've defeated more of the rebels, since yesterday.'

'Praise be,' I say. I don't ask her how she knows. 'What were they?'

'**Baptists**. They had a stronghold in the Blue Hills. They **smoked them out**.'

'Praise be.'

Sometimes I wish she would just shut up and let me walk in peace. But I'm **ravenous** for news, any kind of news; even if it's false news, it must mean something.

We reached the first barrier, which is like the barriers blocking off roadworks, or dug-up sewers: a wooden crisscross painted in yellow and black stripes, a red **hexagon** which means Stop. Near the gateway there are some lanterns, not lit because it isn't night. Above us, I know, there are floodlights, attached to the telephone poles, for use in emergencies, and there are men with machine guns in the **pillboxes** on either side of the road. I don't see the floodlights and the pillboxes because of the wings around my face. I just know they are there.

What details here reveal what Gileadean society is like?

Behind the barrier, waiting for us at the narrow gateway, there are two men, in the green uniforms of the Guardians of the Faith, with the crests on their shoulders and berets: two swords, crossed, above a white triangle. The Guardians aren't real soldiers. They're used for routine policing and other **menial** functions, digging up the Commander's Wife's garden for instance, and they're either stupid or older or disabled or very young, apart from the ones that are **Eyes incognito**.

This term makes them sound important, as if they are protecting the state's religion.

These two are very young: one moustache is still sparse, one face is still blotchy. Their youth is touching, but I know I can't be deceived by it. The young ones are often the most dangerous, the most fanatical, the jumpiest with their guns. They haven't yet learned about existence through time. You have to go slowly with them.

Do you think younger people generally are like this? Why might older people be less so?

Last week they shot a woman, right about here. She was a **Martha**. She was fumbling in her robe, for her pass, and they thought she was hunting for a bomb. They thought she was a man in disguise.

▲ Guards in pillboxes watch the handmaids go into town

GLOSSARY

demurely: as if she is very pure and innocent

orthodox: conventional, officially approved

Baptists: a nonconformist Christian group

smoked them out: made them come out of hiding

ravenous: starving

hexagon: six-sided shape

pillboxes: small defensive buildings with slits for firing guns

menial: humble, lowly

Eyes incognito: special state spies in disguise

Martha: domestic servant in a Commander's household (from the Bible)

SKILLS FOCUS

✔ Explore the theme of social control.

✔ Understand the narrator, Offred.

LOOK CLOSER

1 What impression do you get of Gileadean society from the extract? Consider:
- ○ how the women dress, and what they say to each other
- ○ how the 'barrier' is described
- ○ what happened to the Martha.

2 What impression do you get of Offred? Copy and complete the table below to help you explore her character:

Quotation	Effect
'the notion is absurd'	She is intelligent and critical of the regime.
'like a trained pig's on its hind legs'	She may take pleasure in mentally ridiculing …
'I can't take the risk.'	
'Sometimes I wish she would just shut up …'	

3 What do you think daily life is like for the Handmaids? Consider:
- ○ what restrictions are placed on them
- ○ how far they can express their individuality
- ○ how much they are able to interact with others.

NOW TRY THIS

1 Imagine you are one of the young Guardians at the barrier. Write about the two Handmaids approaching with their passes. You could include:

- ✪ what they see; for example, 'Here they come, their bright red dresses almost to the ground …'
- ✪ how they feel about the Handmaids; for example, 'They're weird. Who knows what's going on in their heads?'
- ✪ any suspicions they might have; for example, 'This one's quite tall. Could it be a man in disguise?'

2 The Handmaids have very restricted lives. Write about the ways you feel your own life is restricted by having to dress, speak or behave in particular ways.

FAST FINISHERS

Write about how you might try to cope with daily life if you were Offred. For example, how might a Handmaid find out if her shopping partner is a 'real believer' or a rebel?

3 Discuss how likely you think it is that our society could become 'dystopian'. Consider:
- ✪ what restrictions there are on people, and how these might increase
- ✪ 'dystopian' developments that could occur, such as overpopulation or climate change
- ✪ what has happened in other modern societies, such as Nazi Germany.

❓ PRACTICE QUESTION

Explore how Atwood presents the theme of the individual and society. You could write about:

- ✪ how the Handmaids are encouraged to behave
- ✪ Offred's secret rebelliousness, revealed in her narrative
- ✪ the Guardians' role as protectors and controllers.

You could begin with: 'The Handmaids are very limited in how far they can express themselves as individuals. For example, …' [8 marks]

◀ Handmaids are trained at The Rachel and Leah Center (also known as the Red Center), named after the biblical sisters Rachel and Leah whose story inspired the role of the handmaids as breeders in Gilead

8 Fahrenheit 451

by Ray Bradbury

▶ Book burning is historically associated with censorship. This photo shows Hitler Youth burning books in 1938

CONTEXT

The title of the novel comes from the temperature at which book paper catches fire and burns (Fahrenheit being the old way of measuring temperature, named after the man who invented the mercury thermometer). It is set in an imagined future world in which most books are illegal. People are still allowed to read cartoons. In the novel, the job of firemen (they are all men) is not to put out fires, but to burn houses that contain books. The owners are imprisoned.

Rather than reading, people sit in their homes surrounded by giant TV screens covering their walls. The programmes are all mindless light entertainment, calculated to fill the heads of the population and prevent them from thinking about anything more challenging, including the purpose of their lives.

In this society, it is also illegal to drive too slowly. In fact, the other form of entertainment seems to be to drive around aimlessly at life-threatening speeds.

The hero of the book, Guy Montag, is a fireman who initially enjoys his work, loving to see houses burn. However, meeting an independent-minded young woman makes him question this, and he begins to take books home with him illegally, and read them. The extract begins at a point when his crime has been reported and he finds himself being ordered by the Fire Chief, Beatty, to torch his own home. Beatty is speaking at the start of the extract.

Book burning has historically been a means of censoring and suppressing information or ideas which are considered to be undesirable. In the 1930s, a Nazi book-burning campaign targeted books by Jewish, communist and other authors considered to be anti-Nazi. *Fahrenheit 451's* author, Ray Bradbury, was also influenced by the censorship and persecution of any suspected communist sympathisers by the US Government in the 1950s, led by Senator Joseph McCarthy.

'Ready.' Montag snapped the safety-catch on the flame-thrower.

'Fire!'

A great nuzzling **gout** of flame leapt out to lap at the books and knock them against the wall. He stepped into the bedroom and fired twice and the twin beds went up in a great simmering whisper, with more heat and passion and light than he would have supposed them to contain. He burnt the bedroom walls and the cosmetics chest because he wanted to change everything, the chairs, the tables, and in the dining-room the silverware and plastic dishes, everything that showed that he had lived here in this empty house with a strange woman who would forget him tomorrow, who had gone and quite forgotten him already, listening to her Seashell radio pour in on her and in on her as she rode across town, alone. And as before, it was good to burn, he felt himself gush out in the fire, snatch, **rend**, rip in half with flame, and put away the senseless problem. If there was no solution, well then now there was no problem, either. Fire was best for everything!

'The books, Montag!'

The books leapt and danced like roasted birds, their wings ablaze with red and yellow feathers. And then he came to the parlour where the great idiot monsters lay asleep with their white thoughts and their snowy dreams. And he shot a **bolt** at each of the three blank walls and the vacuum hissed out at him. The emptiness made an even emptier whistle, a senseless scream. He tried to think about the vacuum upon which the nothingness had performed, but he could not. He held his breath so the vacuum could not get into his lungs. He cut off its terrible emptiness, drew back, and gave the entire room a gift of one huge bright yellow flower of burning. The fire-proof plastic sheath on everything was cut wide and the house began to shudder with flame.

'When you're quite finished,' said Beatty behind him. 'You're under arrest.'

The house fell in red coals and black ash. It bedded itself down in sleepy pink-grey cinders and a smoke plume blew over it, rising and waving slowly back and forth in the sky. It was three-thirty in the morning. The crowd drew back into the houses; the great tents of the circus had slumped into charcoal and rubble and the show was well over. Montag stood with the flame-thrower in his limp hands, great islands of perspiration drenching his armpits, his face smeared with soot. The other firemen waited behind him, in the darkness, their faces illuminated faintly by the smouldering foundation.

Montag and his wife, Mildred, were not close. Now she has left him.

He seems to express himself through fire, and to feel satisfaction in destroying everything connected to a life that he found unsatisfying.

Many people have earpiece radios on much of the time, helping to distract them from thinking for themselves.

Refers to the giant screens that Mildred liked to have on all the time.

Seems to refer to how superficial and trivial he found the broadcast programmes.

How does this flower metaphor make it seem he feels about what he is doing?

Remember: he is under arrest for possessing books.

This personification (as if the house is going to bed) is poetic, as if Montag has created something beautiful by burning the house.

Another metaphor: it has been like a circus for the neighbours – a spectacle to watch.

Montag started to speak twice and then finally managed to put his thought together.

'Was it my wife turned in the alarm?' Beatty nodded. 'But her friends turned in an alarm earlier, that I let ride. One way or the other, you'd have got it. It was pretty silly, quoting poetry around free and easy like that. It was the act of a silly damn snob. Give a man a few lines of verse and he thinks he's the Lord of all Creation. You think you can walk on water with your books. Well, the world can get by just fine without them. Look where they got you, in slime up to your lip. If I stir the slime with my little finger, you'll drown!'

Montag could not move. A great earthquake had come with fire and levelled the house and Mildred was under there somewhere and his entire life under there and he could not move.

> Mildred reported her husband – resulting in her own home being burnt. Do you find this strange?

> These are Christian references. The 'Lord of Creation' is God, and it was Jesus who is said to have walked on water. What therefore is Beatty's attitude towards books?

> Montag is strangely detached. No literal earthquake has taken place. Montag has burnt the house and he now feels as if his old life is in smoking ruins. He feels paralysed.

GLOSSARY

gout: literally a splash of blood

rend: tear up

bolt: sudden flash, like lightning

SKILLS FOCUS

✔ Understand characters and their feelings.
✔ Explore how the dystopian world of the novel is shown.

LOOK CLOSER

1. What do you learn about Montag's attitude towards what he is doing? Consider:
   - what is said explicitly about his feelings as he burns his house
   - the language used to describe, from his viewpoint, what he does and sees.

2. How does the author describe the fire and its effects? What is the effect of the description? Copy and complete the table below to explore this.

Quotation	Effect
'A great nuzzling gout of flame leapt out to lap at the books'	The word 'gout' connects the flame to blood, making it seem more dangerous. Yet 'nuzzling' and 'lap' make it sound like an affectionate and relatively harmless animal.
'simmering whisper'	'Whisper' personifies the fire …
'The books leapt and danced like roasted birds'	

3. What is Beatty's attitude to Montag's crime? How do we know this? Consider:
   - what he says
   - the author's language.

NOW TRY THIS

1 Write an explanation of:
- ✪ what happens in this extract
- ✪ how each man seems to feel.

2 Copy and complete the spidergram, adding your own ideas and associations for 'fire'.

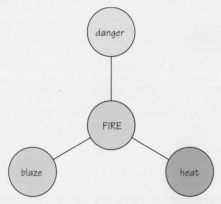

3 Describe someone burning something they feel strongly about. Use language to suggest their feelings, as Ray Bradbury does in the extract, rather than just telling the reader what their feelings are. They could be burning:
- ✪ books they object to
- ✪ things that represent something in their life they want to free themselves from
- ✪ a symbolic object – such as an effigy of Guy Fawkes.

Decide what is being burnt, and why. You do not have to agree with the person's reasons. Try to bring the flames to life using well-chosen adjectives and verbs, and one or two powerful images, as in the extract.

FAST FINISHERS

Write a poem or a prose description of fire from the viewpoint of the fire itself. You could begin with something like this: 'I begin with the hiss of a match bursting into life like a flower. Then …'

4 Discuss what you think has been the significance of books, and the printed word in other forms, in our society. What would our lives be like if books were illegal? Might you rebel, like Guy Montag, and read in secret?

❓ PRACTICE QUESTION

Explore how Bradbury describes the power of fire in the extract. You could write about:
- ✪ the details he includes
- ✪ his use of imagery (for example, 'danced like roasted birds …')
- ✪ his word choice and its effect
- ✪ what fire seems to symbolise.   [8 marks]

9 Seven Years Solitary
by Edith Bone

▲ Edith Bone (1889–1975)

CONTEXT

Edith Bone was born in Hungary in 1889, lived in Germany for ten years, and married an Englishman in 1934. She was a member of the Communist Party of Great Britain. She was working in Hungary as a correspondent for the London *Daily Worker* newspaper when she was arrested by the Hungarian State Protection Authority and accused of spying for Britain. She refused to make a false confession, so was held without trial in solitary confinement in Hungary for seven years. She was freed during the Hungarian Revolution of 1956.

While in prison, Bone devised many different ways of occupying her mind and passing the time in order to avoid becoming mentally ill from her prolonged solitude. One of them is described in the extract. She also preserved her mental health by persistently defying the prison governor and guards, never allowing herself to become a passive victim of the system.

At the end of August 1951, I decided to go on a language strike. I had so many minor disagreements with the staff that I cannot exactly remember what the occasion for it was; it was something connected with the withholding of needle and thread, or the confiscation of a button that had come off some article of clothing – in any case, a trifle. I had no idea what I was starting, when one day I declared that I would speak their barbaric lingo no more.

I suppose I did it partly out of sheer boredom. At any rate I suddenly announced that I would not speak any more Hungarian. I was not a Hungarian subject, I was under no obligation to know the language. It had been a matter of courtesy on my part that I had consented to speak Hungarian at all, and this consent I would now withdraw. I would speak German, or French, or English, or Russian, or Italian; I even offered the doctor Latin –

What impression does this give you of what the prison authorities are like?

Bone's politely 'consenting' to speak Hungarian suggests that she still has some personal power in her relationship with the prison authorities.

Her command of languages might make the guards respect her or even feel inferior to her.

He evidently felt that as a doctor he ought to know Latin, but didn't.

which greatly embarrassed him – but nothing on earth could induce me to speak a word of Hungarian.

For some mysterious reason, which I cannot quite understand to this day, the authorities were seriously worried by this. Possibly there had been fresh enquiries about me just then. First the doctor tried to persuade me. He said: 'Look here, you are damaging your own interests. You may be wanting something, and how can the guards understand you if you speak only English or some other language and not Hungarian?' I answered him in various languages, but not in Hungarian. He denied knowing any other language, which was totally untrue.

The British government may have been trying to find out about her.

Much later, by the way, he claimed to know Russian, but that was not true either. I tested it by talking to him in Russian and saying the most abominable things to him, all in colloquialisms; he nodded very amiably and said 'Da, da,' from which I saw that he had not understood a word of all the unpleasant things I had said to him. The same applied to French, but German he knew quite well.

What makes this funny (especially the word 'amiably')?

She must have been very strong-willed. 'Game' suggests that she was entertaining herself.

I played this game for four and a half months, during which many funny things happened.

One day the governor came in and said to me: 'You know, I have come to the conclusion that you are obviously afraid of something or somebody. Somebody must have been threatening you. Who it was, I don't know, but it is I who am in command here, and nothing can happen here without my permission. Surely you must know that. I give you my solemn word of honour that I will protect you. Not a hair of your head shall be touched, however much Hungarian you speak. So you need not be afraid any more, and may speak freely.' He even went so far as to put his arm round my shoulder in an attempt to convince me that his protection would be efficacious.

I was greatly amused by this and carried on with my strike. I evolved a language of signs, and, when I wanted something, made drawings out of breadcrumbs rolled out into very thin cylinders, from which I shaped the outline of the thing I required.

She is imaginative and creative.

The governor has certainly changed his tune. Perhaps he is just trying a new method.

When it was obvious that I could not be persuaded to speak, I was one day hauled upstairs to the medical room, where the governor suddenly yelled at me in a very brutal tone and threatened me with dire consequences if I did not stop playing the goat. But he got nowhere with this attempt at intimidation. I jumped to my feet, raised my voice, clenched my fists, and gave him such a blast of good Billingsgate that, although he did not know a word of English, he must have understood that I was being extremely rude, and that his threats had done little good.

She is an assertive woman, and is familiar with London's working class.

GLOSSARY

trifle: something unimportant

barbaric lingo: uncivilised language

I was under no obligation: it was not in any way my duty

a matter of courtesy: something done only out of politeness

induce: persuade

abominable: awful

colloquialisms: popular informal phrases

da: Russian for 'yes'

efficacious: effective

dire consequences: awful results (possibly punishments)

playing the goat: behaving foolishly

good Billingsgate: rough and insulting style of speech (possibly with swear words) such as might be used by stallholders in Billingsgate Fish Market in London's East End

SKILLS FOCUS

✔ Understand the narrator's character and attitude.

✔ See how she expresses her attitude to authority.

LOOK CLOSER

1. What do you think is Bone's attitude towards the prison authorities? Copy and complete the table below to help you explore this.

Quotation	Effect
'a matter of courtesy'	By speaking Hungarian only out of considerate politeness, she shows that she sees herself as being in a position of power.
'nothing on earth could induce me to speak a word of Hungarian'	She is completely …
'I played this game for four and a half months'	

2. What impression do you get of Bone's character? Consider:
   - her refusal to speak Hungarian
   - how long she keeps up her 'language strike'
   - how she responds to the governor.

3. What impression do you get of the governor? Consider:
   - his different methods of trying to get Bone to speak Hungarian
   - what pressures he might be under.

NOW TRY THIS

1 In your own words, explain why Bone behaves in the way she does in this extract.

2 Write a letter that the prison governor might write to the Hungarian Minister for Prisons about Edith Bone and his treatment of her. You could begin like this:

> Dear Sir/Madam
>
> I have tried a number of approaches to break down the resistance of the British spy. For example, …

3 Imagine you are in Edith Bone's situation and that escape is impossible. Write a story about one day in prison and what you do to try to stay sane and keep your self-respect. You could begin with your waking up, or with a guard bringing you breakfast.

FAST FINISHERS

Explain why being in solitary confinement for so long would be a psychological strain.

4 In a small group, discuss what you think about solitary confinement as a punishment. Is it cruel? How well do you think you would cope with it yourself? Who in your group would cope best?

❓ PRACTICE QUESTION

Choose **four** statements below which are **true**.

✪ Copy out the ones that you think are true.

✪ Choose a maximum of four true statements.   [4 marks]

A Bone is frightened of the governor.   ☐

B Bone can speak seven languages.   ☐

C Bone is visited by a doctor.   ☐

D Bone gets to speak to other prisoners during exercise time. ☐

E Bone shows evidence of being creative.   ☐

F The governor always treats Bone kindly and courteously.   ☐

G Bone gets bored in prison.   ☐

H The doctor speaks fluent Latin.   ☐

10 An Evil Cradling

by Brian Keenan

▲ Brian Keenan

LEARNING OBJECTIVES

✪ To explore how character is revealed through narrative
✪ To explore the theme of dystopian social and political control
✪ To identify the writer's purpose and viewpoint

CONTEXT

Brian Keenan was born in Belfast in 1950, and is an Irish citizen. He was working as a teacher at a university in Beirut, in Lebanon, when he was kidnapped by Islamic Jihad in 1986. He was kept in solitary confinement for the first two months of the four and a half years that he was held. Then he was put in a cell with another hostage, British journalist, John McCarthy. He was usually kept blindfolded, and was chained hand and foot when not in solitary confinement. He was released in 1990. His account of the ordeal, *An Evil Cradling*, was published in 1991.

This extract is taken from a point in the account a few weeks into his imprisonment. He has decided to go on hunger strike until he is given information about why he is being held, how long he will be held for, and what efforts his captors are making to speak to the Irish Government.

I was amazingly calm. I had not lost that **defiant** self-confidence but for some reason, whether it was the effect of a long period without food or the mind fixing itself so **definitively** on its purpose, I felt no need for anger or aggression. My stubbornness had **interiorized** itself. The guard left, telling me he would return with his chief.

The next morning, after I had been brought back from washing, my kidnapper and a man I presumed to be his boss came to my cell. The chief stood just inside the door while the kidnapper squatted beside me and talked to me. His chief would say something to him in Arabic. He would translate it for me. I would answer but he never translated the answer. I was sure that his chief spoke English and knew exactly what I was saying, but for some reason, and this was to happen again and again, the chiefs when they came would not let their voices be heard speaking English. I repeated

His 'purpose' is to remain on hunger strike.

again what I had earlier told him, so that this boss might hear my reasons and my purposes. I spoke slowly and calmly. I recall that this seemed to cause them some concern. They were probably worried that I was already becoming ill. They explained that they had no doctor. I answered that I did not want a doctor. If they brought one I would refuse to see or speak with him. I was made to stand, then to sit, then to walk in the passage. I assumed my light-headedness and my weakness were obvious to them, for they quickly brought me back to the cell and told me to eat. I refused. They said that I would die. I simply shrugged. I was then told that they did not care if I died, there were many hungry people in Lebanon. I said 'Feed them with this food, for I shall not eat it.' Words were exchanged between the chief and the young kidnapper and they left, saying simply 'OK, you die.' I smiled.

The next day, they were back, the young kidnapper and the prison chief and The Grim Reaper. They checked that my day's ration of food was untouched. Again the question 'Why you don't eat?' I answered, 'I will not eat until you tell me *why*?' They talked outside my cell. For a moment I thought that they would try to punish me, but I was beyond caring. The young guard came back and told me that he did not know, it was simply his job to do such things. I told him that I still wanted to know and would not eat until I was told. He left, and as the door closed I heard him speak outside the cell. I knew that his chief was standing there, listening and saying nothing.

For the next few days nothing happened and I ate nothing. I was confident, I was strong-willed and almost ecstatic as I pushed each meal from me. Occasionally one of the guards would come and tempt me with an apple. But I was beyond desire. Things would come flying through the grille. A piece of cheese, and different pieces of food. I remember carrots were occasionally flung at me. I laughed and laughed. Here was a game I was winning; I was in control and control could not be taken from me.

They take his slow, calm speech as a sign of illness. He is no use to them if he gets sick and dies.

How would you sum up Keenan's attitude, and that of his captors? Do you think they both entirely mean what they say?

This is a popular humorous nickname for death, pictured as a hooded man carrying a scythe to cut down corn (or lives). Perhaps Keenan cheers himself up by giving this nickname to one of his captors.

He uses a *tricolon* – the rhetorical technique of listing three things. ('Ecstatic' means wildly happy.) This and the verb 'pushed' make Keenan sound determined.

This is slightly comic, partly because it echoes the Bible story of the serpent tempting Eve with an apple from the Tree of Knowledge, and then Eve offering it to Adam.

Notice how he calls his strike a 'game', like Edith Bone in Extract 9. This final sentence makes him sound strong.

▲ One of the guards tempts Brian with an apple, echoing the story of the Garden of Eden in the bible

GLOSSARY

defiant: willing to fight or challenge authority

definitively: decisively, purposefully

interiorized: connecting deeply to something within

ecstatic: wild with joy/eagerness

SKILLS FOCUS

✔ Understand Keenan's character and mood.

✔ Explore his narrative technique.

LOOK CLOSER

1 What impression do you get of Keenan's character? Consider:

- ☼ what he does
- ☼ what he says
- ☼ how he describes himself and his captors.

2 How does the passage reveal Keenan's state of mind or mood? Copy and complete the table below. Add at least one more quotation.

Quotation	What it says about Keenan's state of mind
'I had not lost that defiant self-confidence but … I felt no need for anger or aggression.'	He seems to have reached a state in which he can be strong and offer passive resistance without simply reacting to his captors.
'They said that I would die. I simply shrugged.'	He shows that …
'I was beyond caring.'	

3 How is there an element of humour in the final paragraph? Consider:

- ☼ what the guards do
- ☼ how Keenan responds.

NOW TRY THIS

1 Write a paragraph explaining as fully as you can why Keenan goes on hunger strike.

2 Write what one of Keenan's guards (not a 'boss') might write in a diary commenting on Keenan and his hunger strike, and on the role he is playing in guarding him. You could start like this:

> We are all starting to get worried about the prisoner …

3 Imagine you are making a film about Keenan being held captive. Copy and complete the table below to make notes on how details from the extract could be used in the film. Add at least two more details.

Detail	Use in film
'I was made to stand, then to sit, then to walk in the passage.'	Have the actor playing Keenan get up very stiffly and awkwardly. Perhaps have him stagger as he stands, and the guard reach out to steady him …
'They checked that my day's ration of food was untouched.'	Guard lifts a metal lid off Keenan's plate. Close-up on …
'I pushed each meal from me.'	

FAST FINISHERS

Imagine you are on hunger strike like Keenan. Describe how a guard tempts you with your favourite food, and how you struggle to resist.

4 Discuss the differences in situation and type of resistance between Brian Keenan in this extract and Edith Bone in Extract 9. Who do you think is worse off, and why?

❓ PRACTICE QUESTION

What do you learn about Keenan in this extract? Use evidence from the text to back up your findings. Consider:

- ⊙ his character
- ⊙ his coping strategy
- ⊙ how he regards his captors. [8 marks]

11 Final dispatch from Homs

by Marie Colvin

▲ Marie Colvin (1956–2012)

LEARNING OBJECTIVES

- ⊗ To explore the theme of dystopian political control
- ⊗ To identify the writer's purpose and viewpoint
- ⊗ To understand implied meaning

CONTEXT

Homs is a Syrian city that was besieged by the government forces of President Bashar al-Assad from May 2011 to May 2014, during the ongoing civil war. Marie Colvin (1956–2012) was a British–American journalist who worked as a foreign correspondent for *The Sunday Times*. She died shortly after writing this dispatch. The siege ended in a government victory over the opposition. The report is 'dystopian' in that Assad is a dictator, Syria is not a democracy, and the population in the rebel-held cities live such difficult and insecure lives.

> The opening concisely sums up the situation – where, who and for how long.

They call it the widows' basement. Crammed amid makeshift beds and scattered belongings are frightened women and children trapped in the horror of Homs, the Syrian city shaken by two weeks of relentless bombardment.

Among the 300 huddling in this wood factory cellar in the besieged district of Baba Amr is 20-year-old, Noor, who lost her husband and her home to the shells and rockets.

> Focuses on one individual. Why do you think Colvin does this?

'Our house was hit by a rocket so 17 of us were staying in one room,' she recalls as Mimi, her three-year-old daughter, and Mohamed, her five-year-old son, cling to her abaya.

> Shows how the frightened children depend on her, especially in the use of the word 'cling'.

'We had had nothing but sugar and water for two days and my husband went to try to find food.' It was the last time she saw Maziad, 30, who had worked in a mobile phone repair shop. 'He was torn to pieces by a mortar shell.'

For Noor, it was a double tragedy. Adnan, her 27-year-old brother, was killed at Maziad's side.

Everyone in the cellar has a similar story of hardship or death. The refuge was chosen because it is one of the few basements in Baba Amr. Foam mattresses are piled against the walls and the children have not seen the light of day since the siege began on February 4. Most families fled their homes with only the clothes on their backs.

Gives a sense of urgency.

The city is running perilously short of supplies and the only food here is rice, tea and some tins of tuna delivered by a local sheikh who looted them from a bombed-out supermarket.

A baby born in the basement last week looked as shell-shocked as her mother, Fatima, 19, who fled there when her family's single-storey house was obliterated. 'We survived by a miracle,' she whispers. Fatima is so traumatised that she cannot breastfeed, so the baby has been fed only sugar and water; there is no formula milk.

A simple sentence conveys the awful uncertainty.

Fatima may or may not be a widow. Her husband, a shepherd, was in the countryside when the siege started with a ferocious barrage and she has heard no word of him since.

The widows' basement reflects the ordeal of 28,000 men, women and children clinging to existence in Baba Amr, a district of low concrete-block homes surrounded on all sides by Syrian forces. The army is launching Katyusha rockets, mortar shells and tank rounds at random.

Snipers on the rooftops of al-Ba'ath University and other high buildings surrounding Baba Amr shoot any civilian who comes into their sights. Residents were felled in droves in the first days of the siege but have now learnt where the snipers are and run across junctions where they know they can be seen. Few cars are left on the streets.

This mixed metaphor conveys a sense of large numbers of people being cut down. The word 'drove' technically refers to cattle being herded. It is as if the people are slaughtered like cattle.

Verb choices give a sense of the violence of the attack.

Almost every building is pock-marked after tank rounds punched through concrete walls or rockets blasted gaping holes in upper floors. The building I was staying in lost its upper floor to a rocket last Wednesday. On some streets whole buildings have collapsed – all there is to see are shredded clothes, broken pots and the shattered furniture of families destroyed.

How does this appeal to the senses?

It is a city of the cold and hungry, echoing to exploding shells and bursts of gunfire. There are no telephones and the electricity has been cut off. Few homes have diesel for the tin stoves they rely on for heat in the coldest winter that anyone can remember. Freezing rain fills potholes and snow drifts in through windows empty of glass. No shops are open, so families are sharing what they have with relatives and neighbours. Many of the dead and injured are those who risked foraging for food.

It seems a cruel irony that just trying to keep from starving got them killed.

Marie Colvin, *Sunday Times*, 19 February 2012

GLOSSARY

abaya: a robe-like dress worn by some Muslim women

sheikh: Arab chief or leader

obliterated: wiped out

formula milk: manufactured milk for babies

barrage: bombardment of shelling

Katyusha rockets: rockets fired from multiple launchers on trucks

mortar shells: explosive bombs launched from a portable tripod-supported pipe

sniper: a rifle marksman who shoots to kill individuals

foraging: going out looking for whatever food can be found

SKILLS FOCUS

✔ Understand what situation is described.

✔ Analyse how Colvin makes the human situation come to life.

LOOK CLOSER

1. What do you learn about the situation of people in Homs? Consider:
   - where they are
   - what threats they are under
   - possible outcomes.

2. What is Colvin aiming to do in this passage? Consider:
   - the information she gives
   - her choice of details
   - her language – including any emotive language appealing to our sympathies.

3. How does Colvin's word choice create a strong sense of what life in Homs is like? Copy and complete the table below to help you consider this. Add at least one further quotation or detail.

Quotation/Detail	Effect
'Crammed amid makeshift beds and scattered belongings ...'	This shows there is little room ('crammed'), that they have to make do with what little they have ('makeshift'), and that it is quite chaotic ('scattered').
'He was torn to pieces by a mortar shell.'	The emotive 'torn to pieces' shows the violence and ...
'Fatima is so traumatised that she cannot breastfeed'	

NOW TRY THIS

1 Explain in your own words, and by using evidence from the text, how Colvin creates such a strong impression of the awful conditions in which the women and children are living.

2 Imagine you are a mother in the basement telling Colvin your story. Write what you would say. Include:

- ✪ how you came to be there
- ✪ how your children are coping
- ✪ what you all eat
- ✪ how you keep your spirits up.

You could begin like this:

> When the shelling started, we were all terrified ...

FAST FINISHERS

To your answer to question 2, add what you hope for after the civil war has ended.

3 Discuss how you think you would cope psychologically and physically in the basement. What would be difficult? Would you risk going out to look for food?

❓ PRACTICE QUESTION

Choose **four** statements below which are **true**.

- ✪ Copy out the ones that you think are true.
- ✪ Choose a maximum of four true statements. **[4 marks]**

A The basement gives shelter to women and children. ☐

B The women all support the government. ☐

C It is always hot in Syria. ☐

D Colvin shows sympathy for the women and children. ☐

E The women can always get food from the supermarket. ☐

F The snipers mostly shoot from the rooftops of tall buildings. ☐

G Food was hard to come by in Homs during the siege. ☐

H Colvin was in Syria when the siege of Homs ended. ☐

12 Hiroshima

by John Hersey

▲ A child's drawing of Hiroshima victims

CONTEXT

The USA dropped nuclear bombs on the Japanese cities of Hiroshima and Nagasaki in August 1945, ending the Second World War. Germany had already surrendered in May, but Japan had fought on. On 26 July 1945, the Allies threatened Japan with 'prompt and utter destruction' if they did not surrender. Japan ignored this threat, and Hiroshima was bombed on 6 August – the first ever use of a nuclear weapon. When Japan still did not surrender, the USA dropped a second bomb on Nagasaki.

The USA had been a neutral country, not engaging in the Second World War, until Japan bombed the US Pacific fleet in Pearl Harbor in 1941. The Japanese had done this because of existing trade and territorial tensions between the two countries, and to prevent the USA from interfering in Japan's planned expansion in the Far East.

The Hiroshima and Nagasaki bombings killed between 129,000 and 226,000 people, mostly civilians. It is impossible to be precise because many people died of radiation sickness weeks after the bombing, or of cancer or other diseases caused by radiation years later. Radiation is an invisible energy that causes changes to the cells of the body over a period of time.

American novelist and essayist, John Hersey, (1914–93) wrote his book *Hiroshima* in 1946. It is based on interviews with victims, including Mr Tanimoto featured in the extract, who was two miles from the centre of the explosion when it occurred. Like the rest of Hiroshima's population, he was not aware that a nuclear bomb had been dropped (rather than a conventional one) so was baffled by the extent of the devastation. In addition, no one at the time knew how to treat radiation sickness.

Mr Tanimoto, fearful for his family and church, at first ran toward them by the shortest route, along Koi Highway. He was the only person making his way into the city; he met hundreds and hundreds who were fleeing, and every one of them seemed to be hurt in some way. The eyebrows of some were burned off and skin hung from their faces and hands. Others, because of pain, held their arms up as if carrying something in both hands. Some were vomiting as they walked. Many were naked or in shreds of clothing. On some undressed bodies, the burns had made patterns – of undershirt straps and suspenders and, on the skin of some women (since white repelled the heat from the bomb and dark clothes absorbed it and conducted it to the skin), the shapes of flowers they had had on their kimonos. Many, although injured themselves, supported relatives who were worse off. Almost all had their heads bowed, looked straight ahead, were silent, and showed no expression whatever.

After crossing Koi Bridge and Kannon Bridge, having run the whole way, Mr Tanimoto saw, as he approached the centre, that all the houses had been crushed and many were afire. Here the trees were bare and their trunks were charred. He tried at several points to penetrate the ruins, but the flames always stopped him. Under many houses, people screamed for help, but no one helped; in general, survivors that day assisted only their relatives or immediate neighbours, for they could not comprehend or tolerate a wider circle of misery. The wounded limped past the screams, and Mr Tanimoto ran past them. As a Christian he was filled with compassion for those who were trapped, and as a Japanese he was overwhelmed by the shame of being unhurt, and he prayed as he ran, 'God help them and take them out of the fire.'

He thought he would skirt the fire, to the left. He ran back to Kannon Bridge and followed for a distance one of the rivers. He tried several cross streets, but all were blocked, so he turned far left and ran out to Yokogawa, a station on a railroad line that detoured the city in a wide semicircle, and he followed the rails until he came to a burning train. So impressed was he by this time by the extent of the damage that he ran north two miles to Gion, a suburb in the foothills. All the way, he overtook dreadfully burned and lacerated people, and in his guilt he turned to right and left as he hurried and said to some of them, 'Excuse me for having no burden like yours.' Near Gion, he began to meet country people going toward the city to help, and when they saw him, several exclaimed, 'Look! There is one who is not wounded.' At Gion, he bore toward the right bank of the main river, the Ota, and ran down it until he reached fire again. There was no fire on the other side of the river, so he threw off his shirt and shoes and plunged into it. In midstream, where the current was fairly strong, exhaustion and fear finally caught up with him – he had run nearly seven miles – and he became limp and drifted in the water. He prayed, 'Please, God, help me to cross. It would be nonsense for me to be drowned when I am the only uninjured one.' He managed a few more strokes and fetched up on a spit downstream.

Mr Tanimoto climbed up the bank and ran along it until, near a large Shinto shrine, he came to more fire, and as he turned left to get around it, he met, by incredible luck, his wife. She was carrying their infant daughter. Mr Tanimoto was now so emotionally worn out that nothing could surprise him. He did not embrace his wife; he simply said, 'Oh, you are safe.'

A common early symptom of radiation sickness.

The bomb blast burned off many people's clothes.

They seem to be in shock.

Does it surprise you that they seemed unable to relate to the suffering of strangers?

His reaction to being unhurt seems very Japanese, though even in Britain 'survivor guilt' is a recognised feeling.

How would you feel if you were him?

This is a remarkable coincidence. He must be in a severe state of shock not to react more to finding her.

GLOSSARY

lacerated: badly cut

spit: a bit of land extending into the river

Shinto shrine: a holy place of a major Japanese religion

SKILLS FOCUS

✔ Understand the apparent effects of the nuclear bomb.

✔ Explore Mr Tanimoto's experience and feelings.

LOOK CLOSER

1 What effects of the nuclear bomb are described? Consider:

- ✪ people's injuries
- ✪ what the bomb does to clothing
- ✪ the damage to the city.

2 How does Mr Tanimoto react to the bomb? Consider:

- ✪ his worries
- ✪ what he does
- ✪ his feelings.

3 How do other people react? Consider:

- ✪ how they respond to strangers
- ✪ their manner and behaviour.

Copy and complete the table below to help you explore this. Add one more quotation.

Quotation	What it shows
'Many, although injured themselves, supported relatives who were worse off.'	They are caring towards family members.
'... heads bowed, looked straight ahead, were silent, and showed no expression whatever.'	It seems the experience is too overwhelming for them ...
'people screamed for help, but no one helped'	

NOW TRY THIS

1 Imagine you are in Hiroshima after the explosion. Write your own account of what you experience, based on Mr Tanimoto's experience. You could begin like this:

> People were streaming past me, mostly silent and expressionless …

2 Write a government-issued list preparing people for what they can expect in the event of a nuclear attack.

FAST FINISHERS

Make up a newspaper headline and opening paragraph for an article on the Hiroshima attack. Assume that the newspaper is based in a nearby city but that, as a reporter, you have been able to speak to people like Mr Tanimoto.

3 In small groups, discuss:

- ✪ your view of the USA's decision to drop nuclear bombs on Hiroshima and Nagasaki. (Re-read the *Context* box for the background relations between the USA and Japan.)
- ✪ the pros and cons of countries such as Britain, the USA, Russia and North Korea having nuclear weapons now.

❓ PRACTICE QUESTION

Write a plan for an essay arguing either for or against the view that major nations should possess nuclear weapons to deter other nations from attacking them with their own nuclear weapons. Here are some tips:

- ✪ Plan an introduction explaining the question.
- ✪ Make your case for or against the view.
- ✪ Consider the counter-arguments to your own view and explain why you do not find them sufficiently persuasive.
- ✪ Think of a gripping opening and a strong, clear conclusion.
- ✪ Consider how you will use facts, and perhaps emotive language. [8 marks]

◀ The ruin of the Hiroshima Prefectural Industrial Promotion Hall still stands today despite being located directly below the explosion. It is kept to serve as a reminder of the war and is part of the Hiroshima Peace Memorial Park

13 Chernobyl
by Serhii Plokhy

LEARNING OBJECTIVES

- ✪ To explore how character is revealed through narrative
- ✪ To explore the theme of dystopian society
- ✪ To analyse the writer's language choices

▶ Alexey Akindinov's painting "Chernobyl. Last day of Pripyat" (120x180 cm, oil on canvas, 2013-2014) shows the disaster at the Chernobyl nuclear power plant on April 26, 1986

CONTEXT

The Chernobyl disaster is the worst nuclear accident in history. It occurred in a power plant in the Ukraine (then part of the Soviet Union, led by Russia) on 26 April 1986. A safety test being done on an RBMK reactor, a type of reactor commonly used in the Soviet Union, went wrong. Such reactors use a radioactive fuel, uranium, to create a nuclear reaction, which creates heat. This turns water into steam, which then turns a turbine that generates electricity.

During the test, the reactor became dangerously unstable, but the senior engineer was determined to complete the test and ordered it to continue. At the point when it seemed too dangerous, operators tried to shut down the reactor, but the design fault meant that this led to a steam explosion instead. This destroyed the reactor core and created a fire that raged for nine days.

The work of the firefighters was far more dangerous than they realised, because of the radioactive materials spread by the explosion, and the high levels of radioactive emissions where they were working. They all suffered from radiation sickness, and some died, either within weeks, or years later due to related illnesses.

Major Tellatnikov was running out of time. He sent reinforcements to the roof of reactor No. 3. By 3.30 am, he, too, was experiencing the symptoms he had seen in the firefighters he had sent to the hospital only an hour earlier: nausea and retching. It was his turn to be taken to the hospital.

By now, the Shavrei brothers Leonid and Ivan, who were both at the power plant fighting the fire, had been joined by their younger brother, Petr. Leonid was on the turbine hall, and Ivan had been sent to the top of reactor No. 3 with those who were replacing the Pravyk and Kibenok crews. Petr had arrived with another off-duty officer to help deal with the fire. He was not even wearing his gear when, approaching the turbine hall, he heard the voice of his brother, Leonid, who was shouting, 'Give me hoses; there are no hoses!' The hoses he was using had been burned by the melting **bitumen**. 'I immediately took off my shoes and put on **kersey boots**, throwing my cap into the car,' recalled Petr. 'I put two hoses under my arms and climbed the ladder to the top. And that was all the protective gear I had – just my boots! Protection didn't matter – minutes counted to stop the flames from spreading.'

The new hoses were finally on the roof of the **turbine** hall, but there was no water. With the electricity gone, the plumbing system that was supposed to supply water to the pumps was dead. Petr Shavrei made a decision on the spot – to use water from the cooling pond nearby. It was easier said than done. Around him was a scene from the **Apocalypse** – the concrete blocks, window glass, **graphite**, and fragments of fuel rods, all thrown up by the blast, created a hellish obstacle course for the trucks that had to get to the pond. 'I ran in front of the truck – there was no lighting; everything was covered with debris,' remembered Petr. 'I dodged like a rabbit, with the truck following me. And still the wheels were punctured. I took metal rods out of the wheels with my hands and kicked them out with my feet. Then the skin peeled off my hands – the metal rods were radioactive.' Eventually they managed to reach the pond. Water was delivered to the roof of the turbine hall, and the fire was again brought under control.

It was only closer to 7.00 am, when the fire was finally extinguished, that the Shavrei brothers were allowed to leave their positions around the damaged reactor. Ivan, who had been fighting the fire on the top of reactor No. 3, was taken away by an ambulance. He had a sweet taste in his mouth and could barely stand up. Leonid climbed down from the roof of the turbine hall on his own, but he was vomiting. Petr, who had arrived last, already did not feel well: 'I was retching and felt terribly weak. My legs wouldn't respond, as if they were made of cotton,' he remembered. What he wanted most was a drink. He reached for a water hose and drank from it, experiencing immediate relief. 'What are you doing, it's dirty!' said a fellow crew member, referring to the water brought from the cooling pond. Petr responded that the water looked clean. 'But the water was **radioactive** – I knew that, but it seemed to me that if I didn't get a couple of swallows, I would fall and wouldn't be able to get up,' Petr recalled. He would pay dearly for those two sips of water from the Chernobyl pond – his **digestive tract** was severely damaged.'

Usually the first sign of radiation sickness. The firefighters had not been trained in fighting a nuclear fire, and at first thought they were just being affected by smoke.

Even off-duty firefighters were helping. What does this tell you?

Responding to the urgency of the fire means he has even less protection against radiation.

The steam and the hot water that the power plant created would normally be cooled by this pond.

How is this metaphor appropriate?

The firefighters did not understand at the time that the debris was radioactive, but Petr knew this by the time he gave this account.

Both symptoms of radiation sickness.

This final sentece has a dramatic effect because it shows that something so small had a terrible effect.

▲ Today, there is still an exclusion zone around the Chernobyl disaster site. It is one of the most radioactively contaminated areas in the world

GLOSSARY

bitumen: oil-based product used on flat roofs (at Chernobyl) and roads

kersey boots: long leather boots used by Russian army

turbine: machine which produces power by being rotated (in this case by steam)

Apocalypse: end of the world

graphite: a mineral, a form of carbon

radioactive: a substance which gives out invisible ionising (destabilising) atomic particles that damage cells in the body

digestive tract: gut

SKILLS FOCUS

✔ Understand the challenge faced by the firefighters.
✔ Explore the author's narrative technique.

LOOK CLOSER

1 What problems did the firefighters face? Consider:
- ✪ the urgency of the situation
- ✪ radioactivity and how well they were prepared for it
- ✪ the water situation.

2 How does the writer bring the situation to life? Copy and complete the table below. Add at least one further quotation from the extract.

Quotation	What it shows
'Major Tellatnikov was running out of time.'	This topic sentence creates a sense of urgency.
'Protection didn't matter – minutes counted to stop the flames from spreading.'	Using a firefighter's words …
'a hellish obstacle course'	

3 What is the impact on the reader of Petr drinking from the hose? Consider:
- ✪ how he must have felt at the time
- ✪ how likely you might be to drink from a fire hose normally
- ✪ the final sentence of the extract.

NOW TRY THIS

1 Sum up in your own words the firefighters' attitude towards putting out the fire.

2 Write the start of a story in which a number of people carry out dangerous emergency work for the good of others. For example, you could choose from:

- ✪ a rescue from a flooded cave
- ✪ a mountain rescue
- ✪ looking for earthquake survivors.

FAST FINISHERS

Firefighters at Chernobyl carried on working even after realising the dangers of radiation. Write a letter recommending that one or more of them should be given an award for bravery. In it, explain what they did and why they deserve the award. You could begin with:

Dear Comrade,

I wish to commend the brave actions of [name one or more firefighters] at Chernobyl power plant ...

3 In a small group, discuss your views on whether nuclear power should still be regarded as a good alternative to other ways of generating electricity, given what happened at Chernobyl.

❓ PRACTICE QUESTION

Choose **four** statements below which are **true**.

- ✪ Copy out the ones that you think are true.
- ✪ Choose a maximum of four true statements.　　　　　　　　　[4 marks]

A The firefighters have been trained in fighting a radioactive fire.　☐

B Petr Shavrei has reason to regret drinking from the fire hose.　☐

C Petr Shavrei only starts to fight the fire once he is in full kit.　☐

D An early symptom of radiation sickness is nausea.　☐

E Three of the firefighters are brothers.　☐

F One of the firefighters refuses to go close to the fire.　☐

G One symptom of radiation sickness is a bitter taste in the mouth.　☐

H The firefighters use water from the reactor's cooling pond.　☐

14 Ghosts of the Tsunami

by Richard Lloyd Parry

▲ The tsunami left a trail of destruction in its wake

LEARNING OBJECTIVES

- ✪ To explore narrative technique
- ✪ To explore the theme of dystopia shown in a disaster
- ✪ To identify the writer's purpose and viewpoint

CONTEXT

On 11 March 2011, a powerful undersea earthquake off the coast of Japan created a 14-metre-high tsunami (a huge wave) that caused devastation as it swept inland, killing more than 22,000 people. It also caused a disaster at the Fukushima nuclear plant – the worst nuclear accident since Chernobyl (see Extract 13).

This extract gives an account of Teruo Konno, an earthquake expert working in the Ishinomaki town hall, who was blown out of his office by the force of the tsunami. The town hall had received warning of the tsunami and Konno was preparing to deal with it. Landing in the rushing water, he was swept inland, then back towards the sea when the tsunami reached its furthest extent inland and began to suck back out – like an ordinary wave hitting the beach, but on a massive scale.

Konno returned to his desk. The speed of events was difficult to grasp. Until moments ago, he had been leading a trained team in the execution of a well-rehearsed and rational plan. Now he, and all those around him, were facing death. The forces acting on the building were pushing it to the extremes of its resistance. The ground floor was completely underwater; now the wave was rising through the upper floor. Konno climbed onto his desk, as black water sucked and slapped around it with violent force. Then there was another, immense percussion, and suddenly he was tumbling through open air.

The outside world was cold; Konno had the sensation of falling through it very slowly. He was able to take in the sight of the building from which he had just been propelled, with water surging out of all its windows. He was aware of another colleague, a man named Abe,

Air pressure from the wave hitting the building must have forced him through the office window.

Time can seem to slow down at a time of emergency like this. Why do you suppose that is?

falling through space alongside him: the image of Abe's surprised, bespectacled face lodged in his mind. Then he was in the water.

It was churning and raging with violent internal motion. Konno described it as 'like being in a washing machine'; he was paralysed by the water's grip. He was aware of having been forced down, and of touching asphalt – the surface of the car park, which was now the bottom of the sea. And he understood that his life was coming to its end. 'It's true what people say. You see the faces of your family, of your friends. It's true – I remember it. All those faces. The last words in my mind were, "I'm done for – I'm sorry." It's a feeling different from fear. Just a frank feeling of sorrow, and regret.'

As he was viewing the gallery of his past, Konno found himself able to move his neck, and then his arms and legs and, kicking and thrashing, he propelled himself upwards and broke the surface.

He cast around for something to hold on to. A tree branch came into his grip, but it was too small. He exchanged it for a thicker spar of timber. On the surface, he could make out Abe, minus his glasses, gripping onto a sturdy log and being carried north, away from the river and towards the hills. But Konno was spinning in the opposite direction, towards what had been the river and was now the sea. Having faced death without fear, now he became afraid. 'It was like being sucked into a whirlpool,' he said. 'I went under again, and again I thought this must be the end. And then, somehow, I was released from it, and I was in the middle of the river in a slow and quiet stream.'

He caught hold of a wide wooden panel, the section of a house's outer wall, a stable support compared to the rotating tree branches. Gripping this, he drifted steadily towards the bank again and the hills that rose out of the flood. He could tell, more or less, where the submerged embankment and road must be; he imagined lowering his feet in the shallower reaches and wading to safety. But just as hope was returning, the tsunami began to withdraw, and the stampeding waters reversed direction.

Konno found himself being carried back out into the stream and towards the river's mouth. Familiar landmarks passed at racing speed. He saw the outline of his office building – it had not collapsed after all. Clinging to his raft, Konno was rushed downstream by the withdrawing tide, through the river's gaping mouth and out towards the horizon of the Pacific Ocean.

The phenomenon of 'your life flashing before your eyes' is one that has often been reported by people who think they are about to die.

Like a series of pictures in an art gallery.

What does this metaphor make the tsunami sound like? What is the effect on the reader?

The short simple sentence, following on from the image of bespectacled Abe, is like time suddenly returning to normal speed. Try to picture it as if in a film.

This emphasises how everything has been transformed – a car park is now the sea bed.

The currents of the tsunami seem very unpredictable.

The river is made to seem like a monster. What is the effect of this personification?

SKILLS FOCUS

✔ Understand what happens to Konno.
✔ Explore the writer's technique.

LOOK CLOSER

1 Create a storyboard showing the key stages of what happens to Konno. Include captions and either sketches or illustration briefs, as shown below.

Caption	Illustration
'Konno climbed onto his desk'	A worried man climbing onto a desk in a flooding office.
'… suddenly he was tumbling through open air.'	Konno in mid-air, the raging water below, broken windows and shattered glass …
'Then he was in the water.'	

2 What is the meaning and effect of these phrases?

Quotation	Meaning and effect
'black water sucked and slapped'	The water creates currents and waves within the office. The onomatopoeia of 'sucked and slapped' make it seem alive.
'another, immense percussion'	
'churning and raging'	
'stampeding waters'	

3 How do Konno's feelings change during the course of the extract? Find quotations to back up your ideas.

NOW TRY THIS

1 Write a paragraph summarising what happens to Konno in the extract.

2 Imagine the building you are in has been hit by a tsunami. Write about your experience. Try to make your description come alive by careful choice of details and vocabulary. You could:

- ✪ use some imagery, like the personification in this extract in 'the water's grip', the simile in 'It was like being sucked into a whirlpool' or the metaphor in 'stampeding waters'.
- ✪ use language that appeals to the senses (for example, 'sucked and slapped')
- ✪ use surprising details, like the car park in the extract becoming the bottom of the sea.

FAST FINISHERS

Write the beginning of a news feature on the tsunami hitting the building you are in. Start by making up a headline like the ones below:

GIANT WAVE CAUSES
DEVASTATION

HOW I SURVIVED
A TSUNAMI

THE DAY THE SEA CAME
TO MY SCHOOL

3 In pairs, discuss what important memories from your life would flash before your eyes if you were in a time of crisis. You could begin by thinking of three memories each.

❓ PRACTICE QUESTION

How does the writer make Konno's experience of the tsunami come alive for the reader in the extract? You could write about:

- ✪ the details chosen
- ✪ language that appeals to the senses
- ✪ well-chosen vocabulary, such as active verbs (for example, 'tumbling')
- ✪ imagery. [8 marks]

15 Review of *Blade Runner*

by Robert Osborne, in the *Hollywood Reporter*, 1982

▲ Harrison Ford in the 1982 film, *Blade Runner*

CONTEXT

Blade Runner had mixed reviews when first screened, but it is now seen as a classic dystopian science-fiction film. It stars Harrison Ford, who had already made a name for himself in two *Star Wars* films and *Raiders of the Lost Ark*. He plays Rick Deckard, a bounty hunter. It was directed by Ridley Scott, whose other films include *Thelma and Louise*, *Gladiator* and *The Martian*. The film was made in 1982. Although set 37 years into the future (2019), its mood owes a lot to the corrupt world of crime novels of the 1940s and 1950s with their tough, cynical detective heroes.

Welcome to Ridley Scott's nightmare. Resembling a **Felliniesque** journey into **Dante's Inferno**, with **Mickey Spillane** in tow, *Blade Runner* is a cold, bold, bizarre and **mesmerizing** futuristic detective thriller that unites the British-born director of *Alien* with new box-office dynamo Harrison Ford for results that are as impressive as any film that's exploded through a projector so far this year.

Admittedly, it's a film that will turn off many, but it will also bulge eyeballs and cause talk. And since talk sells tickets, the Ladd Company release, made in association with Sir Run Run Shaw and going out via Warner Bros., can hardly avoid making a marketable impression.

Blade Runner is not an easy film to watch comfortably, or categorize smoothly. It possesses a size that is awesome, sound and visual accompaniments that blasts the senses, and a pessimistic attitude that would do justice to the hellish worlds Josef von Sternberg investigated in his Germanic and Paramount projects in the early 1930s.

Punchily sums up the writer's viewpoint using rhyme, alliteration and assonance, and reveals the film's genre.

The metaphor makes it sound exciting and full of impact.

The physical image has more impact than saying 'it is visually impressive'.

A list of three (a triplet or tricolon) makes a powerful impression of the film's qualities.

Like Von Sternberg, Scott packs the screen ratio at every turn with images that penetrate. Overall, the concept is likewise chilling.

Set 37 years in the future in 2019 Los Angeles, a time and place within the potential reach of many of today's moviegoers, Scott doesn't promise much to anticipate. In his view, the City of Angels has become a ghoulish circus of towering, pyramid-like buildings, flying cars, space stations and a constant barrage of TV commercial hype writhing on the sides of monstrous buildings and from blimps endlessly careening through an air that's dense with searchlights, smoke, smog and dust. Rain is a constant.

At ground level, streets are crowded with bodies, and much of the city has become Oriental. Bright neons entice. Steam billows from all compass points. Underneath all is a constant sense of claustrophobia, hopelessness and terror. (It is some comfort that the downtown Million Dollar theatre seems to still be playing Spanish films in 2019, and Hare Krishna members are still out there parading the streets in their yellow sheets.)

Within this haze, Harrison Ford narrates a tale with all the world-weariness of a spent Sam Spade, with dialogue by screenwriters Hampton Fancher (who co-executive-produced with Brian Kelly) and David Peoples straight out of such film noir cop classics as *Murder, My Sweet* and *The Brasher Doubloon*. Ford is an ex-Blade Runner, once a paid assassin of 'replicants', the latter of a genetically engineered breed of 'humans' now outlawed on earth.

When four 'replicants' manage to return to earth, Ford is enlisted by the police to find them, and terminate them. *Blade Runner* follows Ford's trail through the L.A. jungles as he accomplishes his mission, namely the destruction of Joanna Cassidy, Brion James, Daryl Hannah and Rutger Hauer. Adding to his problem is the fact that Sean Young, with whom he is having a romantic alliance, may also be a dreaded 'replicant.'

It all adds up to a virtual feast for sci-fi devotees, not to mention audiences who appreciate decidedly off-beat themes and substance worth debate. For them all, Blade Runner will require more than one visit to get all the implications.

Many people watching the film in 1982 would still be alive in 2019, when the film is set.

Abstract nouns convey the mood of the film.

Hare Krishna is a Hindu religious group whose members chant in praise of the god Krishna.

This cleverly combines information on character, mood and production.

What do you think using 'terminate' rather than 'kill' suggests?

Sums the film up as unusual, worth discussing and worth seeing more than once to understand what it suggests about future society.

GLOSSARY

Felliniesque: in the style of Italian film director, Federico Fellini, known for films blending fantasy, bizarre images and the down-to-earth

Dante's Inferno: Dante was a medieval Italian poet who wrote a famous narrative poem of this name depicting hell

Mickey Spillane: popular US gritty crime novelist, first published in 1947

mesmerizing: hypnotic, fascinating

Josef von Sternberg: Austrian–American film director (Germany and Hollywood) known for emotional intensity and gangster movies

ghoulish: macabre, horrific

blimp: large wingless aircraft consisting of a gas-filled balloon, carrying passengers in a suspended basket

careen: speed forward while also moving side-to-side

bodies: people – not dead bodies

Oriental: an outdated term that meant relating to Asian people and culture

neons entice: neon lights lure passers-by (for example, into bars)

compass points: directions

spent: weary, exhausted

Sam Spade: detective main character of Dashiell Hammett's 1930 novel *The Maltese Falcon*

film noir: genre of film featuring pessimistic, cynical or corrupt characters, especially detectives and criminals

off-beat: quirky, unusual

SKILLS FOCUS

✔ Understand the writer's viewpoint.

✔ Explore the use of critical language.

LOOK CLOSER

1. From what you now know about the dystopian genre, how does the opening paragraph make it clear that *Blade Runner* is a dystopian film? Consider:
   - what it is compared with
   - the language used.

2. The review is very favourable. (The reviewer loves the film!) What phrases especially suggest this, and how? Copy and complete the table below. Select and add at least one more quotation.

Quotation	Effect
'… bold, bizarre and mesmerizing'	Suggests that the film takes risks, is very unusual, and will completely absorb its viewers.
'as impressive as any film that's exploded through a projector'	The powerful verb 'exploded' …
'it will also bulge eyeballs and cause talk'	

3. The reviewer cleverly works information on the production of the film into his description of what the film is like. Find and quote two examples of this.

NOW TRY THIS

1 Re-read paragraphs 5 and 6 of the review (from 'Set 37 years ...'). Using details from these paragraphs, and more of your own, write a paragraph introducing the character of Rick Deckard (Harrison Ford) and the setting of L.A. You could begin like this:

> *Rick Deckard wove through the neon-lit sea of people ...*

2 Make notes on what details you might include if you were making a dystopian film set in Britain in 2057. You could consider these areas:

- ✪ effects of climate change
- ✪ technology – for example, how will people travel?
- ✪ the role of computers, electronic devices and robots
- ✪ government and policing
- ✪ a good title for the film.

3 Sketch or make design notes for a poster advertising your film. Begin with an exciting line that could go straight after the title to grab readers' attention and whet their appetite for the film.

FAST FINISHERS

Imagine your dystopian film has been made. Write at least the start of a review introducing and praising your film. Aim to tell readers what the film is about and what you think of it.

4 In small groups, discuss what you think life in Britain will really be like 37 years from now. You could consider the bullet points in question 2 and whether you think there are ways in which life will be better; for example, there could be advances in medical science. Finish by taking a vote on whether you think life will be better or worse overall.

❓ PRACTICE QUESTION

Explore how the review writer makes readers aware of how L.A. is depicted in the film. Consider the use of:

- ✪ details
- ✪ language
- ✪ literary techniques
- ✪ different sentence types and lengths. [8 marks]

▲ Viggo Mortensen and Kodi Smit-McPhee in the 2009 film adaptation

LEARNING OBJECTIVES

⊗ To explore why the writer has made certain language choices
⊗ To explore the theme of dystopia in a film
⊗ To identify the writer's purpose and viewpoint

CONTEXT

This is a review of the film *The Road* in *The Spectator*, a broadly right-wing (Conservative-leaning) magazine commenting on politics and culture. Boris Johnson is one of its current journalists. The review gives the context of the film. For more context, see page 5 in the introduction section.

Bear in mind the purposes of a film review are to:

⊗ inform people thinking of going to see a film
⊗ interest people who have seen the film and wonder if the reviewer has similar views to theirs
⊗ inform and entertain people who are interested in cinema, or culture generally
⊗ help readers to engage in discussion with other film-goers.

A character in Joseph Conrad's novel *The Heart of Darkness* comments on life with these words. This would appeal to readers who recognise the quotation. The reviewer entertains us by treating the subject flippantly (not seriously).

As if she is being reluctantly dragged back to the film.

Sets the tone of much of the review: wittily tongue-in-cheek rather than deadly serious, like the film.

The Road is based on Cormac McCarthy's post-apocalyptic novel and, as far as roads go, this one is long, hard, brutal, pitiless and profoundly horrible, plus there doesn't seem to be much reward for sticking with it. It is very much like the North Circular in all these respects, unless you count finally getting to Ikea as a reward, which no one in their right mind would. 'The horror, the horror,' as Joseph Conrad would surely have said, if he'd found himself in Ikea on a Saturday afternoon. He might also have added: 'And the meatballs are rubbish,' but we'll just never really know.

But here? With this road? OK, here we have a father (Viggo Mortensen) and his 8-year-old son (Kodi Smit-McPhee) who appear to be among the last survivors of some unspecified cataclysm. We don't know what disaster has struck – nuclear?; environmental? – only that

Again, she is joking, but also commenting on the clichés of films like this.

Jokily presents this as one of the horrors.

Short, simple sentences give the feeling that she is grudgingly listing the film's good points.

Sums up her view of the film.

it has, and now the earth is washed up, pretty much. The landscape is wrecked. Trees eerily creak and then crash to the ground. Random fires burn. An obscured sun casts a dingy, brown light. Everything is blanketed in a choking ash. Abandoned cars festoon the highways as, post-apocalyptically, they always do. (Just once, I would like a post-apocalyptic film to feature balloons.) Only a few flashbacks refer to a time before, when the world was in colour, the boy was a baby, and there was a mother on the scene, as played by a glowing, golden Charlize Theron, who at least had the sense to check out early.

The man and his son are seeking the sea, if only because it gives them some purpose. The father is scared of not being able to protect the boy. The boy is scared that his father is losing his humanity, will stop being one of the 'good guys'. All other survivors seem to be bad guys, particularly the terrifying cannibals who rove in gangs like flesh-eating zombies from a horror movie. The journey is one of desperate scavenging punctuated by moments of acute danger, various horrors – vomiting, coughing blood, severed heads, puddles of guts – and having Robert Duvall turn up as an all-but-dead old lump named Eli, giving it all a faintly religious, Old Testament tone. Adapted by the British playwright Joe Penhall, and directed by John Hillcoat (who made the slickly violent *The Proposition*), this is an endurance test as much for us as for those on screen, but to what end? We're being asked to sit through this for why, exactly?

This film is not badly done. Most of it, in fact, is well done. The dying, blighted earth is hauntingly and chillingly captured. There are powerfully affecting moments. We feel the paternal bond. Mortensen and Smit-McPhee are magnificently intense. But? It just isn't satisfying in any way, probably because it shrinks from answering its own questions. Can humankind retain its decency once stripped of everything else? Is man's nature essentially savage? And, ultimately, it doesn't answer the question Charlize asked just before she so sensibly checked out: what is the point of going on? As I have not read the book – give us a break, I'm behind with *Come Dine With Me* as it is — I cannot say how faithful this is but, having read other McCarthy books, would say the novel probably repaid your attention with its astonishing prose. This, though, puts you through the wringer, but doesn't repay you in any way. This was always going to be a bravely non-commercial film – which, you can bet, will mean it'll be hailed as a masterpiece in some quarters — but it's mostly a monotonous slog. This road goes nowhere, which is better than Ikea, but it is nowhere all the same.

What is the effect of this informal language?

Grimly ironic humour, referring to the mother deciding to end her life rather than try to survive in this post-apocalyptic world.

Uses rhetorical questions to express the view that the film is pointless.

Returns to humour. If she is (jokingly) prioritising *Come Dine With Me* – a popular TV show, what must she expect the book to be like?

Gives a sense of completion by returning to her earlier joke, and makes a final serious point.

GLOSSARY

post-apocalyptic: set in an imagined time following a global disaster transforming life as we know it

North Circular: ring road around North London

Ikea: a large Swedish-based chain of stores selling flat-pack furniture, etc.

cataclysm: disaster

festoon: decorate, adorn (used ironically – they are not really very pretty)

Robert Duvall: older famous actor with a small role in the film

paternal: fatherly

puts you through the wringer: metaphor meaning 'makes you suffer emotionally'

SKILLS FOCUS

✔ Understand the reviewer's views on the film.
✔ Explore the writing style and its purpose.

LOOK CLOSER

1. What aims does the reviewer seem to have? Look again at the *Context* section. Find examples of how she is fulfilling the purposes in the bullet list there.

2. What does the reviewer think of the film? Consider:
   - what she says are its good points
   - her criticisms
   - her conclusion.

3. How does the reviewer vary her tone for different effects? Copy and complete the table below. Add at least one more phrase or sentence.

Quotation	Effect
'long, hard, brutal, pitiless and profoundly horrible'	The string of adjectives seriously sums up the experience of being in the world of the film, telling the reader that this is not exactly enjoyable.
'unless you count finally getting to Ikea as a reward'	Undermines the previous sentence, suggesting that …
'Just once, I would like a post-apocalyptic film to feature balloons.'	

NOW TRY THIS

1 Write an alternative ending to the first paragraph, beginning with 'It is very much like ...' Consider these options:

- ✪ think of a different road and destination
- ✪ think of a different simile altogether – perhaps something long, painful and pointless, possibly including an 'unless you count ...'
- ✪ think of a more serious comparison.

2 Write a review of a film that you have watched but not enjoyed. If necessary, make one up. Include:

- ✪ what the film is about
- ✪ who stars in it and anything you want to say about their performances
- ✪ your views on the film, including at least one positive point.

FAST FINISHERS

Explain what types of film you most enjoy and why. Give some examples.

3 Discuss how a dystopian film could paint a grim picture and yet still in a sense be entertaining or enjoyable. Begin by thinking of any dystopian films you have seen, or any films you have seen that some people might say were depressing, or too pessimistic to enjoy – perhaps including war films.

The reviewer, Deborah Ross, found the film unrewarding. In your discussion, you could include what could make a film about sad events 'rewarding'.

❓ PRACTICE QUESTION

'Novels and films should be uplifting and optimistic, rather than painting a negative view of the world or worrying people about the future.'

Write a plan for an essay exploring your views on this statement. You could consider:

- ✪ the purposes of novels and films (for example, to entertain, to make audiences think, etc.)
- ✪ how far you think they should reflect real life
- ✪ any examples you have (real or made-up).   [8 marks]

Poetry

17 Not My Business
by Niyi Osundare

▲ In a dictatorship, the justice system is also corrupt

LEARNING OBJECTIVES

⊕ To explain the writer's language choices
⊕ To explore the writer's use of structure
⊕ To see how texts fit into their cultural and historical settings

CONTEXT

Nigerian-born Osundare is a dramatist, literary critic and university professor as well as being a poet. He is known for championing freedom of speech and has often publicly criticised the President of Nigeria. He now lives in the USA, but while still living in Nigeria he was often questioned and monitored by the security forces because he published poems criticising the government. Osundare has said in an interview:

'You cannot keep quiet about the situation in the kind of countries we find ourselves in, in Africa. When you wake up and there is no running water, when you have a massive power outage for days and nights, no food on the table, no hospital for the sick, no peace of mind; when the image of the ruler you see everywhere is that of a dictator with a gun in his hand … then there is no other way than to write about this, in an attempt to change the situation for the better.' (*The Nation*, 11 June 2017)

Not saying who 'they' refers to makes them anonymous and sinister; 'picked up' makes the soldiers sound casual.

They picked Akanni up one morning
Beat him soft like clay
And stuffed him down the belly
Of a waiting jeep.

'Stuffed' suggests the soldiers' rough, careless treatment of Akanni; how does the 'belly' metaphor then fit with the next stanza?

What business of mine is it
So long they don't take the yam
From my savouring mouth?

They came one night
Booted the whole house awake
And dragged Danladi out,
Then off to a lengthy absence.

Notice the violent verbs.

There is no mention of where he is taken, but the reader can probably guess.

The refrain (repeated stanza) is a rhetorical question suggesting the attitude of the ordinary citizen trying to ignore the dystopian persecution and injustice around them.

What business of mine is it
So long they don't take the yam
From my savouring mouth?

Chinwe went to work one day
Only to find her job was gone:
No query, no warning, no probe –
Just one neat sack for a stainless record.

She has never done anything wrong at work, but now she has to gather her possessions (from her desk?) and carry them away in a sack. She is literally 'getting the sack'.

What business of mine is it
So long they don't take the yam
From my savouring mouth?

Dramatic use of suspense – literally, because his hand is suspended on the way to his mouth. Notice the alliteration linking 'hungry' to 'hand'.

And then one evening
As I sat down to eat my yam
A knock on the door froze my hungry hand.

The silence is sinister. Repetition of 'waiting' emphasises time seeming to slow down.

The jeep was waiting on my bewildered lawn
Waiting, waiting in its usual silence.

This is a transferred epithet: the adjective actually applies to the narrator, but the lawn is seen as bewildered by the presence of the jeep.

GLOSSARY

jeep: off-road vehicle similar to a Land Rover, often used by the military

yam: vegetable which grows underground like a potato; a major part of the diet in some African countries

savouring: slowly enjoying eating

SKILLS FOCUS

✔ Understand the narrator's character and attitude.

✔ Appreciate the poet's use of linguistic techniques.

LOOK CLOSER

1 What do you think is the poet's attitude towards the security forces, as expressed through the narrator's voice? Copy and complete the table below to help you explore this. Add at least one more quotation.

Quotation	Effect
'They picked Akanni up'	The security forces are an anonymous and sinister group, not a number of recognisable or approachable individuals. They treat people casually: beating someone up is 'all in a day's work'.
'What business of mine is it So long they don't take the yam From my savouring mouth?'	The narrator thinks that if he ignores what is happening to others …
'Booted the whole house awake And dragged …'	

2 What is the effect of the phrase 'Beat him soft like clay'? Consider:

- ✪ the impact of the verb choice
- ✪ the simile
- ✪ what the phrase makes you see and feel.

3 What is the effect of the refrain (repeated phrase), 'What business of mine is it / So long they don't take the yam / From my savouring mouth?' Consider:

- ✪ why it uses a rhetorical question
- ✪ what attitude it expresses
- ✪ the effect of naming the food
- ✪ the effect of the verb 'savouring'.

NOW TRY THIS

1 Imagine you are either Akanni or Danladi and have now been released from prison. Tell the story of your arrest. You could begin with:

> *We were all sleeping peacefully when …*

2 Write a news feature about the arrest of either Akanni or Danladi. Choose to write it for:

- a pro-government newspaper, justifying the arrest and speaking positively about the conduct of the security forces involved, or
- a paper that dares to criticise the government and the security forces, treating the arrest as brutal and unjust.

Begin by writing a headline that will sum up the story and your chosen approach. Here are some examples:

> DANGEROUS MILITANT TAKEN
> INTO CUSTODY

> INNOCENT FAMILY MAN BEATEN
> BY SOLDIERS

3 Write the first and second stanzas of a poem using the same structure as 'Not My Business':

- Begin the first stanza with 'They …' followed by something that the security forces did to someone.
- Write a second stanza that could be a refrain (repeated phrase), expressing the same attitude as the one in 'Not My Business'. Begin it with 'What do I care …'

FAST FINISHERS

Write the rest of the poem, ending with what happens to the narrator. Think of a good title for your poem, which could be a phrase included in the poem.

4 In threes, role-play a TV discussion about one of the incidents in the poem, with one speaker justifying it, another criticising it, and one acting as 'chair', making sure that both speakers have their say. The chairperson should try not to take sides in the discussion.

❓ PRACTICE QUESTION

'The poet creates an effective picture of a sinister and unjust system.'

Discuss how far you agree with this view. Consider:

- the message of the poem
- word choice
- imagery
- literary techniques. [8 marks]

▲ Sights like this were a part of everyday life during the Troubles. This vehicle is protected by Kremlin-2 mesh, mentioned in the poem

LEARNING OBJECTIVES

- ✪ To explain the writer's language choices
- ✪ To explore the writer's use of metaphor
- ✪ To see how texts fit into their cultural and historical settings

CONTEXT

Ciaran Carson (1948–2019) was born into an Irish-speaking, working-class Catholic family in Belfast. He went on to become a Professor of English at Queen's University, Belfast. He lived in Belfast during the time known as 'the Troubles'. This was an ongoing conflict focused on members of the Protestant community who wanted Northern Ireland to remain part of the United Kingdom, and members of the Catholic community who wanted it to become part of a united Ireland.

This conflict goes back to 1609, when Scottish and English Protestants were given land taken from the native Irish, in an attempt to make Ireland loyal to the English crown. From the nineteenth century onwards, there was pressure from Irish nationalists to make Ireland an independent country. Eventually, in 1922, 26 out of 32 Irish counties became independent, forming the Republic of Ireland.

During the Troubles, terrorist acts were carried out by paramilitary forces – especially the Irish Republican Army (IRA) on the Catholic side, and the Ulster Defence Association (UDA) on the Protestant side. British Army troops occupied Northern Ireland until 2007. They were often accused of using heavy-handed, repressive tactics, especially by the Catholic community.

In this poem, a British Army 'riot squad' attempts to deal with a disturbance on the streets of Belfast. A nail bomb explodes, scattering what (with grim humour) is termed 'Belfast confetti'. This incident occurred in August 1969. In the same year, the poet narrowly escaped death when a stray bullet hit a taxi he was in.

Narrator establishes the central metaphor comparing the contents of a nail bomb (any small metal objects) with punctuation marks, thus linking language and violence.

An asterisk (*) looks like a tiny explosion.

Punctuation marks that stop the flow of words.

His knowledge of the streets makes the poem personal. Appropriately, they are named after battles, except for Raglan, who was a commander in the Crimean War.

Suddenly as the riot squad moved in, it was raining exclamation marks,

Nuts, bolts, nails, car-keys. A fount of broken type. And the explosion

Itself – an asterisk on the map. This hyphenated line, a burst of rapid fire …

I was trying to complete a sentence in my head, but it kept stuttering.

All the alleyways and side-streets blocked with stops and colons.

I know this labyrinth so well – Balaclava, Raglan, Inkerman, Odessa Street –

Why can't I escape? Every move is punctuated. Crimea Street. Dead end again.

A Saracen, Kremlin-2 mesh. Makrolon face-shields. Walkie-talkies. What is

My name? Where am I coming from? Where am I going? A fusillade of question marks.

A pun: a 'fount' can mean both a fountain (like the contents of the bomb pouring out) and a collection of small metal letters and punctuation marks used in pre-digital printing.

As if he is trying to put words together but is hindered by the confusion of the moment; 'stuttering' could refer to machine-gun fire.

The question and short, simple sentences (two are not even full sentences) reflect frustrated attempts to escape the soldiers.

The narrator is stopped by soldiers 'firing' questions at him.

◄ The Saracen tank became particularly recognisable as a result of its use by the British Army in Northern Ireland

GLOSSARY

labyrinth: colloquially, a maze (for example, of streets); in Greek myth, a place where a dangerous half-human, man-eating creature, the Minotaur, was imprisoned

Saracen: type of tank

Kremlin-2 mesh: a protective wire cage giving extra protection to the tank

Makrolon: a strong, lightweight, bullet-resistant plastic

fusillade: a round of rapid, continuous gunfire

SKILLS FOCUS

✔ Understand the poem's central metaphor.
✔ Explore the poet's word choice and techniques.

LOOK CLOSER

1. What is the mood of the poem? Consider:
   - what event is being described
   - the words and phrases suggesting violence
   - the nail-bomb metaphor
   - how the soldiers are presented
   - the types of sentence used.

2. How does the language of the poem create a sense of violence, danger and entrapment? Copy and complete the table below. Add at least one more quotation.

Quotation	What it says about his state of mind
'it was raining exclamation marks, Nuts, bolts, nails, car-keys'	Exclamation marks are used to express surprise or anger. The metaphor of the metal objects forming them links anger to the violent injury they could do.
'it kept stuttering'	Suggests the narrator's helplessness, as well as …
'I know this labyrinth so well'	

3. Describe the effects of sentence length and punctuation in 'Why can't I escape? Every move is punctuated. Crimea Street. Dead end again.'
   - How does the form of the sentences reflect what they are about?
   - How does the narrator seem to be feeling, and what expresses this?

NOW TRY THIS

1 Imagine you are an eyewitness to the nail bomb exploding. Write an account for a local newspaper. Include:

- ✪ seeing and hearing the bomb going off
- ✪ the effects – for example, injuries
- ✪ the British Army presence (you could include some of their equipment)
- ✪ how local people react to the Army.

2 Now imagine you are a young soldier on tour in Northern Ireland for the first time. You are tasked with preventing a riot, clearing the streets and detaining anyone who seems suspicious. You are also one of the soldiers questioning the narrator. Write a letter home about the experience. You could begin with something like this:

> Dear Mum
>
> I hope you're all well back home. I'm doing OK, but …

3 Write a poem in the voice of either:

- ✪ a British Army soldier involved in the event described in Carson's poem, or
- ✪ the nail bomb itself. You could make it mysterious, not revealing at first who or what is speaking, and you could include the contents of the bomb as listed in Carson's poem. Include at least one metaphor or simile.

Your poem does not have to rhyme.

FAST FINISHERS

Write a short poem beginning 'Why can't you go home?' set during the Troubles, and from the point of view of someone who wants the British Army to leave Northern Ireland.

4 Work in pairs asking each other the kind of questions you think the soldiers would ask passers-by, as in Carson's poem.

❓ PRACTICE QUESTION

How does Carson create a sense of tension and danger in the poem?
Use evidence from the text to back up your answer. Consider:

- ✪ use of detail
- ✪ sentence lengths and types
- ✪ imagery
- ✪ the use of the soldier's 'voice'.   [8 marks]

19 Out of the Blue – 12
by Simon Armitage

▲ The iconic 'Twin Towers' of the World Trade Centre in New York City

LEARNING OBJECTIVES

- To explore the theme of dystopia
- To identify the writer's purpose and viewpoint
- To understand the writer's structural choices

CONTEXT

On 11 September 2001, both towers of the World Trade Centre in New York were hit by planes hijacked by terrorists. These attacks were planned and co-ordinated by al-Qaeda leader, Osama bin Laden, who was killed by the US Army in 2011. A total of 2,753 people died as a result of these attacks. There was a similar attack on the Pentagon in Washington DC on the same day which killed 184 people. A fourth hijacked plane was crashed into a field, killing 40 passengers and crew.

Fires started in both World Trade Centre towers. About 200 people chose to jump from the high windows. Of course, some stood at the windows for some time before doing this. Others stood there just to escape the smoke and heat for as long as possible. One man was seen and filmed waving a shirt from a window. Simon Armitage's poem is narrated from the imagined viewpoint of this man.

Out of the Blue is a long poem which is divided in 13 fragments. Below is one of these fragments, which was included in the poem-film *Out of the Blue*, commissioned by Channel 5 and aired in 2006.

Seems to address both the reader and someone watching, perhaps on TV.

> You have picked me out.
> Through a distant shot of a building burning
> you have noticed now
> that a white cotton shirt is twirling, turning.
>
> In fact I am waving, waving.
> Small in the clouds, but waving, waving.
> Does anyone see
> a soul worth saving?

'Soul' could just mean a person, or could be religious (saving from hellfire). Also suggests 'SOS' ('Save Our Souls').

Repetition seems to prolong the moment, as if the man is just trying to live a little longer. Weak, unstressed line-endings suggest his vulnerability.

78

Seems to address the emergency services, hoping for rescue.

So when will you come?
Do you think you are watching, watching
a man shaking crumbs
or pegging out washing?

I am trying and trying.
The heat behind me is bullying, driving,
but the white of surrender is not yet flying.
I am not at the point of leaving, diving.

What do you think he is 'trying' to do?

A bird goes by.
The depth is appalling. Appalling
that others like me
should be wind-milling, wheeling, spiralling, falling.

Verbs describe how people fall from the towers. Present participles (ending in '-ing') emphasise the present moment as something continuous.

Interesting word choice. Fish breathe through gills. Why do you think the poet uses this?

Are your eyes believing,
believing
that here in the gills
I am still breathing.

'Flagging' means becoming exhausted, but also suggests waving a flag (the shirt). Who might he be addressing in 'my love'?

But tiring, tiring.
Sirens below are wailing, firing.
My arm is numb and my nerves are sagging.
Do you see me, my love. I am failing, flagging.

Rhyme scheme changes to two rhyming couplets (pairs), signalling end of poem, and anticipating the end of the man's life.

◀ Within two hours of the planes hitting the towers, both had collapsed

SKILLS FOCUS

✔ Analyse the poet's word choice.
✔ Analyse the poet's use of form and structure.

LOOK CLOSER

1 Try to summarise what each stanza is about. Consider:
- ✪ what is described
- ✪ word choice
- ✪ who, if anyone, is addressed
- ✪ sentence forms, including questions.

2 Focus on the present participle verbs. They often have a number of associations, rather than just one simple meaning. Copy and complete the table below, adding more present participle verbs from the poem, to explore these associations.

Verb	Possible meaning/associations
'burning'	Danger, urgency. Something can only burn for a while before it is destroyed.
'twirling, turning'	Sound more casual, almost playful, as if the viewer might not have realised the urgency?
'waving'	Has several associations; for example, …
'saving'	

3 What is the effect of the rhetorical question in the third stanza? Consider:
- ✪ how it relates to the reality of the situation
- ✪ what sort of tasks are imagined
- ✪ the irony.

NOW TRY THIS

1 Think of the person who the man might be addressing when he says, 'my love'. Imagine he is able to send this person a final email on a laptop as he stands by the window. Write what he might say. If you prefer, you could write from the viewpoint of a woman. You could, if you wish, begin with one of the following lines:

> It looks like I won't be home for your birthday ...

> I never thought that I would say this, but ...

> Unless there's a miracle ...

2 Write your own poem based on this one, in which a narrator is in a desperate situation, not knowing whether they might be rescued or be able to save themselves somehow, at the last moment. They could be:

- ✪ up a mountain in a storm
- ✪ on a sinking ship or in the sea after it has sunk
- ✪ lost in space or left behind on another planet (for example, Mars).

FAST FINISHERS

Write another poem, or add one or two more stanzas to the poem you have written, in which your narrator is rescued.

3 Discuss what you would remember, think about and what you would try to do if you were in a desperate situation like the man in the poem.

❓ PRACTICE QUESTION

How does Simon Armitage convey a strong impression of the man's experiences in the poem? Plan a response to this question using evidence from the poem. You could write about:

- ✪ how the structure of the poem develops a narrative
- ✪ how language techniques such as repetition are used
- ✪ what language choices the poet makes
- ✪ how the poem makes readers visualise the man's situation. [8 marks]

▲ A 'mushroom cloud' from the atomic bomb dropped on Hiroshima

LEARNING OBJECTIVES

- To explore the theme of dystopia
- To identify the writer's narrative viewpoint
- To understand the writer's structural choices

CONTEXT

On the date in the poem's title, 6 August 1945, the *Enola Gay*, an American Boeing B-29 Superfortress bomber plane (named after the pilot's mother) dropped an atom bomb on Hiroshima, in Japan. This was the first atomic bomb ever dropped. Even the scientists behind its design and construction could not be sure what effect it would have, but in fact, it destroyed virtually all of Hiroshima. A few days later, the Americans dropped a second atomic bomb on another Japanese city, Nagasaki. This forced the Japanese to surrender, bringing the Second World War to a close.

The plane's pilot, Colonel Paul Tibbets, was 30 years old at the time of the bombing. He died in 2007, aged 92, after a post-war career in the Air Force and aviation. Reflecting on Hiroshima, he said:

'I made up my mind then that the morality of dropping that bomb was not my business. I was instructed to perform a military mission to drop the bomb. That was the thing that I was going to do to the best of my ability.'

For further context on what led up to the bombing of Hiroshima, see page 86.

The poet uses imagery to describe three stages of the bombing. The first is the explosion that creates the familiar 'mushroom' cloud. This is compared with a famous photograph of Marilyn Monroe with her white dress being blown up by the warm air coming out of a subway air vent. This dates from 1955: in 1945, Monroe's career was just beginning. The second stage is the firestorm that consumed much of the city, along with 'black rain' – actually radioactive material. The third stage brings the early effects of radiation.

Alison Fell (born 1944) is a Scottish poet and novelist who is especially interested in feminism and politics.

In the Enola Gay
five minutes before impact
he whistles a dry tune

Later he will say
that the whole blooming sky
went up like an apricot ice.
Later he will laugh and tremble
at such a surrender, for the eye
of his belly saw Marilyn's skirts
fly over her head for ever

On the river bank,
bees drizzle over
hot white rhododendrons

Later she will walk
the dust, a scarlet girl
with her whole stripped skin
at her heel, stuck like an old
shoe sole or mermaid's tail

Later she will lie down
in the flecked black ash
where the people are become
as lizards or salamanders
and, blinded, she will complain
Mother you are late. So late

Later in dreams he will look
down shrieking and see

ladybirds
ladybirds

Annotations:

A pun: means both the sky changing colour like a flower, and a colloquial British swearword expressing surprise.

As if he is unconcerned – it is all in a day's work.

Comparing it to something as ordinary as an ice cream implies the pilot's detachment from the event.

Could refer to a viewing window in the 'belly' of the plane through which Hiroshima's destruction could be seen, and to Japan being forced to surrender to America – also like an assaulted woman.

Is he trying to make light of his feelings of guilt or unease?

Suggests the calm of a normal summer's day, about to be shattered.

The girl, skin 'stripped' by the blast to reveal red-raw flesh and muscle, represents all the people of Hiroshima.

As if she is shedding her skin; a dehumanising image, as if her suffering hardly matters.

Refers to 'black rain' – radioactive material falling to the ground.

They shed their skins.

Her mother must be dead but the girl is not thinking rationally. 'Late' also means 'dead'.

Strong, emotive verb suggests the pilot's guilty nightmares.

As in the children's rhyme, 'Ladybird, ladybird, fly away home; your house is on fire, your children are gone.'

▲ The Bombadier's position in the nose of a B-29 bomber

GLOSSARY

drizzle: light rain – here referring to the light touch of the bees

rhododendrons: flowering bushes

salamanders: lizard-like amphibians, thought in medieval times to be born from fire, or to be immune to fire; they also shed their skin

SKILLS FOCUS

✔ Understand the poem's narrative and time frame.

✔ Explore the poet's language techniques and word choice.

LOOK CLOSER

1. Much of the poem is written in the future tense, emphasising how much everything has changed from its starting point 'five minutes before impact'. However, it also includes phrases and sentences with verbs in the present and past tenses. Copy out one example of each tense.

2. Using a ruler on a blank sheet of paper, create a timeline of the poem to show how it moves from before the bomb is dropped, to the present and into the future. Include:

   ✪ the starting point of the poem, at the start of the timeline
   ✪ other moments before the bomb is dropped
   ✪ moments shortly after the bombing
   ✪ the pilot, later – and much later.

   Look at your timeline. Does the poem move forward in a simple chronological time order? How does the poet deal with time? What do you think is the effect?

3. How does the poet's word choice convey meaning? Copy and complete the table below to explore this. Add at least one further quotation.

Quotation	Effect
'impact'	A short, quite technical word conveys the immediacy of the bomb's effect. Also suggests the pilot's detachment from the bomb's likely effect.
'like an apricot ice'	This casual simile, referring to something an American might enjoy on a summer's day, suggests …
'drizzle'	

NOW TRY THIS

1 Imagine you are the pilot of the *Enola Gay*. Based on the poem, write an account of your experience of the bombing from a viewpoint one year after the event. Include:

- ✪ your thoughts and feelings as you fly towards Hiroshima
- ✪ your memory of the event itself
- ✪ your feelings and experience now, a year after the bombing.

2 Write a poem about an important event in your life (real or imagined) that brought about major changes for you and/or other people. Use the same time structure as Alison Fell's poem:

- ✪ begin before the important event; for example, 'On the pitch, five minutes before the goal …'
- ✪ move on to imagining the future, with a line like 'Later, I will say …'
- ✪ move back to the present moment before the event; for example, 'In the crowd, a chant starts up …'
- ✪ move forward to a future point; for example, 'Later, in dreams, I will see the ball again and again …'

FAST FINISHERS

Write a dialogue between the pilot and either a friend or his wife after the mission has taken place and the crew have returned to the USA. They could, for example, discuss:

- ✪ what it was like for the pilot leading up to the bombing, and at the moment of dropping the bomb
- ✪ how the pilot feels about the mission now (perhaps a week later)
- ✪ what they both think it has achieved for America, or the world
- ✪ any worries either of them may have about the event and its consequences.

Lay out your dialogue like a playscript, such as:

| PAUL [pilot] | Hi Dan. *Great to see you. So, what are they saying about me round here?* |
| DAN | *You know, the usual stuff – what a great guy you are – but I just wondered about …* |

3 In small groups, discuss:

- ✪ how far you agree with the pilot's view (see the *Context* section) that someone in the armed forces should not consider the morality of what they are ordered to do
- ✪ what examples you can think of (real or imagined) where a member of the armed forces might say, 'I was just following orders'.

❓ PRACTICE QUESTION

A student has written:

'The poem "August 6, 1945" is very effective in making readers see and feel what a huge, momentous event the dropping of the bomb on Hiroshima was.'

Write a plan for an essay discussing how far you agree with this statement. [8 marks]

▲ A Catholic rosary

LEARNING OBJECTIVES

⊗ To explore the poet's use of narrative
⊗ To explore the theme of dystopian society
⊗ To analyse the poet's language choice

CONTEXT

Midori Nagai was a young Catholic woman who died when the atom bomb was dropped on Nagasaki in 1945. Her husband, Takashi, was a radiologist (a doctor who specialises in diagnosing disease using X-rays). After the war, he became a peace activist. Midori Nagai's rosary (a string of beads used to count prayers – also a symbol of Catholic belief) was melted by the blast, and is now in a museum in Nagasaki commemorating the work of Takashi Nagai.

Rowan Williams is a critic, theologian, philosopher and poet. He is also a former archbishop of Canterbury.

For more context on the dropping of the atom bombs on Japan in 1945, see page 82.

The air is full of blurred words. Something
has changed in the war's weather. The children
(whose children will show me this) have been sent
to the country. In the radiology lab,
Takashi fiddles, listening to the ticking bomb
in his blood cells, thinks, once, piercingly,
of her hands and small mouth, knotting him in
to the long recital of silent lives
under the city's surface, the ripple of blurred Latin,
changing nothing in the weather of death and confession,
thinks once, in mid-morning, of a kitchen floor, flash-frozen.

After the atom bomb was dropped on Hiroshima, Takashi and Midori decided to evacuate their children from the city for their safety. Clearly they survived.

He had leukaemia (cancer of the blood), caused not by the atom bomb but by exposure to radiation through working with X-rays. He knows it will kill him eventually.

This could mean those killed by the atom bomb.

Masses (Catholic services) were spoken in Latin.

Refers to the moment of the bomb blast, at 11.02 a.m.

This stanza is all one complex sentence. The first part follows on from 'When …'; the second explains what happens 'when', and begins with 'the hard things …'

Probably refers to the black radioactive material falling from the sky.

When, in the starburst's centre,
the little black mouth opens, then clenches,
and the flaying wind smoothes down the grass
and prints its news black on bright blinding
walls, when it sucks back the milk
and breath and skin, and all the world's vowels
drown in flayed throats, the hard things,
bone and tooth, fuse into consonants of stone,
Midori's beads melt in a single mass
around the shadow with its blackened hands
carved with their little weeping lips.

Days earlier, in Hiroshima, in what was left
of the clinic chapel, little Don Pedro, turning
from the altar to say, The Lord be with you,
heard, suddenly, what he was about to claim,
seeing the black lips, the melted bones,
and so, he said, he stood, his small mouth
open, he never knew how long, his hands
out like a starburst, while the dialogue
of stony voiceless consonants ground across
the floor, like gravel in the wind, and the two
black mouths opened against each other,

Nobody knowing for a while
which one would swallow which.

The blast created a wind that flattened grass (and buildings). It even flayed some people (removed their skin).

This is Midori herself, burned to death by the bomb blast.

Reveals that he survived to recall this moment.

Visually echoing the shape made by debris being blasted outwards by an explosion.

GLOSSARY

flaying: removing skin

consonants: sounds in words, such as 'b', 'c' and 'd', that are not vowels

SKILLS FOCUS

✔ Understand the poem's narrative.
✔ Explore the author's language techniques.

LOOK CLOSER

1. Try to explain what you think happens in this poem. Consider:
   - ⚬ the lead-up to the Nagasaki bomb blast
   - ⚬ what happens to Midori and her rosary in the blast
   - ⚬ how the poem tracks back in time to the Hiroshima bomb a few days earlier.

2. How does the poet use key words and phrases? Copy and complete the table below. Add further words or phrases from the extract. Bear in mind that there is not always a clear single meaning for each; you will have to interpret what you read.

Quotation	Possible meaning and effect
'blurred words'	Could mean literally hard to hear on the radio; creates a sense of confusion and uncertain information and rumours leading up to the bomb blast.
'ticking bomb'	Suggests the idea of a bomb fitted with a timer device …
'flash-frozen'	

3. How would you describe the mood of the poem? What words and phrases do you think especially create this mood?

4. The title of the poem focuses on Midori's rosary, suggesting that it is an especially important part of the poem's message. If the rosary is a symbol of Catholic belief and prayer, what central message does the poem convey?

▶ The atomic bomb dropped on Nagasaki left the whole city in ruins

NOW TRY THIS

1 Plan a poem which describes someone who dies and leaves behind a very significant object, which could suggest something important about that person, in the way that Midori's rosary does. Begin by drawing a spidergram or mind map with a small image of the object at its centre, like the one started below.

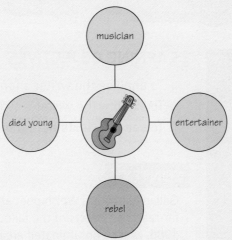

2 Think of an object you have that in some way represents an important part of your own life or identity. Describe the object and explain why it is important and what it says about you.

FAST FINISHERS

Write a poem about an object you chose for questions 1 or 2 above.

3 Discuss what four objects you would choose to represent your life in Britain, at this point in time, that could be placed in a time capsule to be discovered by future generations. Try to reach a majority decision and be prepared to explain your choices as a group.

? PRACTICE QUESTION

Choose **four** statements below which are **true**.

✪ Copy out the ones that you think are true.

✪ Choose a maximum of four true statements.   [4 marks]

A Midori died in Hiroshima.   ☐

B Midori's children survived the bomb blast.   ☐

C Takashi was killed by the blast.   ☐

D Midori was a Catholic.   ☐

E The rosary is used in the poem as a symbol.   ☐

F The poem does not repeat any words.   ☐

G Midori's rosary was perfectly preserved.   ☐

H Don Pedro was a priest.   ☐

▲ Lambs in Wales were affected by radioactivity from Chernobyl

LEARNING OBJECTIVES

⊙ To analyse the writer's language choices

⊙ To explore the writer's structural choices

⊙ To see how texts fit into their cultural and historical settings

CONTEXT

Gillian Clarke is a Welsh poet and playwright. The poem is about the far-reaching effects of the fallout from the Chernobyl nuclear disaster in 1986, which contaminated areas as far west as north Wales. The Soviet Union's refusal to admit to weaknesses in its power plants, together with its system of pressurising individuals to meet targets and deadlines, enabled the accident to happen. Its reluctance to then admit to the world that the accident has occurred meant that there was a delay in other countries being warned about the spread of nuclear fallout on the wind. For more context on the Chernobyl accident, see page 54.

The Chernobyl accident happened at the end of April. Spring was late, so the nuclear fallout had more effect in some ways; for example, there were still newborn lambs on the hills.

Nuclear fallout killed many birds. Some migrating birds reached other countries before dying.

Poland was close to Chernobyl, so was badly affected by fallout. Some of its milk was too dangerous to drink. How might the phrase also relate to the saying about 'crying over spilt milk'?

That spring was late. We watched the sky
and studied charts for shouldering isobars.
Birds were late to pair. Crows drank from the
lamb's eye.

Over Finland small birds fell: song-thrushes
steering north, smudged signatures on light,
migrating warblers, nightingales.

Wing-beats failed over fjords, each lung a sip of gall.
Children were warned of their dangerous beauty.
Milk was spilt in Poland. Each quarrel

Carrion crows eat dead lambs. They peck at their eyes.

Children could have been contaminated by touching birds that had died from fallout.

Refers to 'Pandora's box' in Greek mythology. Prometheus stole fire from the gods, so Zeus, King of the Gods, took revenge by giving Pandora to Prometheus' brother. She opened a jar (mistranslated as 'box'), releasing death and other evils into the world. Nuclear power could be seen as a gift that released unexpected evils.

Refers to firemen who fought the blaze when the nuclear plant exploded (see page 54).

A hopeful image probably referring to the Bible story of Noah and the Flood: when a dove returned with an olive leaf in its beak, Noah knew the water level was going down.

the blowback from some old story,
a mouthful of bitter air from the Ukraine
brought by the wind out of its box of sorrows.

This spring a lamb sips caesium on a Welsh hill.
A child, lifting her head to drink the rain,
takes into her blood the poisoned arrow.

Now we are all neighbourly, each little town
in Europe twinned to Chernobyl, each heart
with the burnt firemen, the child on the Moscow train.

In the democracy of the virus and the toxin
we wait. We watch for spring migrations,
one bird returning with green in its voice,

glasnost
golau glas,
a first break of blue.

Images of 'poisoned' innocence.

Ironically takes the benign (positive, safe) ideas of being neighbourly, and town twinning, and relates them to the effects of Chernobyl.

Democratic because a virus or toxin could affect anyone.

Clarke ends on a positive note, suggesting that some good can come even out of something as bad as the Chernobyl accident.

GLOSSARY

isobars: lines of atmospheric pressure, used to show weather on a chart

Finland: a small country to the east of Russia

fjord: a deep, narrow inlet of the sea

gall: contents of the gall bladder (a bodily organ); very bitter

Ukraine: a country that was once in the western part of the Soviet Union

caesium: an element; caesium 137 is a radioactive material that was released in the Chernobyl accident

glasnost: the move in the Soviet Union, under President Mikhail Gorbachev, towards more open sharing of information (if the Soviet Union had told the rest of the world about the nuclear accident, affected countries could have taken action to tackle the effects of radiation sooner)

golau glas: Welsh for 'blue light'; it could also be taken to mean blue sky – a gap in the clouds

SKILLS FOCUS

✔ Understand the writer's language choices.
✔ Explore the writer's structural choices.

LOOK CLOSER

1. ○ Write headings that would appropriately summarise or represent each stanza.

   ○ Look at your headings. Then write one or two sentences explaining the overall structure of the poem – how it moves from one idea to the next.

2. What is the meaning and effect of these phrases and sentences? Copy and complete the table, adding at least two more quotations of your own.

Quotation	Meaning and effect
'Crows drank from the lamb's eye.'	Crows pecked at the eyes of dead lambs. Although not necessarily the result of fallout, the disturbing image fits the subject of the poem.
'smudged signatures on light'	The birds look 'smudged' because they are moving, but the word also suggests that they are about to be …
'Wing-beats failed over fjords'	

3. How does the poem convey the idea of the innocent victims of the nuclear fallout? Find three examples and explain their effect.

▶ The cooling tower overlooking the Chernobyl nuclear power plant

NOW TRY THIS

1 Write a news feature for a local paper in north Wales based on the information in the poem. You could include:

- ✪ information about the Chernobyl accident
- ✪ what effects have been noticed east of Chernobyl, and why – including raised levels of radiation in Wales
- ✪ warnings – for example, about drinking milk, or about birds.

Begin by thinking of a striking headline, perhaps something like:

> NUCLEAR FALLOUT REACHES BANGOR

> LOCAL MILK UNSAFE TO DRINK, SAYS EXPERT

2 Write *either* two or three stanzas of a poem *or* a prose description about a child finding a beautiful bird that has died from radiation. You could include:

- ✪ what the child is doing when he or she finds the bird – for example, going to school
- ✪ what the bird looks like
- ✪ what the child thinks when discovering the bird
- ✪ what happens next – does the child pick up the bird or not?

FAST FINISHERS

- ✪ Complete your poem or description from question 2.
- ✪ Look at two or three of your word choices and explain why you chose them.

3 Gillian Clarke says: 'Now we are all neighbourly.' In a group, discuss what she means by this and what issues the world faces as a whole, which affect everyone (such as global warming), and how these issues might develop in your lifetimes.

❓ PRACTICE QUESTION

Plan a response to the following question.

A student has written: 'Gillian Clarke has written a poem quietly but effectively expressing her anger over the Chernobyl incident.' Write about how far you agree, using evidence from the poem. You could write about:

- ✪ her choice of details
- ✪ her use of imagery
- ✪ the structure of the poem
- ✪ the poem's overall message.   [8 marks]

23 The Revived Piano

by Hideko Yokota, translated by Ava Yuhki

▲ A piano was dug from the mud in Fukushima and repaired

LEARNING OBJECTIVES

- To explore why the writer has made certain language choices
- To explore the theme of dystopia
- To identify the writer's purpose and viewpoint

CONTEXT

This poem was inspired by the TV news. An earthquake had caused a tsunami (a huge wave) that had led to a nuclear accident and flooded Fukushima in Japan. After the flood had subsided, a piano was dug out of the deep mud and repaired by local volunteers. For more context on the tsunami, see page 58.

The poet was born in Osaka in 1939.

The broken sounds,
covered with mud, writhe and groan.
The legs of the piano, lid and keys
were scattered here and there
and buried –
in resentment against destruction.

The people lamented over
the sorry pieces and
made a vow to the blue sky.

With prayer, picking up the pieces
one by one from the mud,
they put them together
as if completing a puzzle.

> The sounds are personified, as if they echo the suffering of the people.

> The colour blue indicates fine weather, suggesting hope for the future.

> Indicates the difficulty of mending the piano, but could also refer to the puzzle of exactly why the disaster happened.

At the site where once stood a musical instrument shop,

the love for the piano unfolded.

Not just that love,

but that the days before the destruction might be regained.

Let's reply to such a great deal of sorrow

and the voices now vanished.

Seems to indicate a wish, or even a prayer, that things could return to normal.

People who died in the tsunami, appropriately suggested by sound.

The melodies

of the revived piano

are heard beyond the rumbling of the sea –

carried on the winds

beyond the horizon,

and from flocks of seagulls

are delivered to the people on the street.

A reminder of the power of the nearby ocean.

From the orange waves

of drifting safflowers,

a joyous concerto –

Suggests hope and joy being resurrected from the disaster thanks to shared efforts. What might the 'waves' also suggest?

This is the site where they dug the piano

out of the deep mud,

accompanied by

cheerful voices.

A positive, hopeful ending.

GLOSSARY

lamented: grieved, expressed their sorrow

sorry: in this context, sad-looking, broken (not apologetic)

safflower: a plant with orange or yellow flowers, used medicinally and for its edible oil

concerto: a piece of music consisting of three movements, in which either one solo instrument (for example, a violin) or a group of soloists is accompanied by an orchestra

SKILLS FOCUS

✔ Understand the writer's use of symbolism.
✔ Explore the writer's word choice.

LOOK CLOSER

1. Make a list or mind map of words and phrases you associate with 'piano'. If you use a visual means of showing them, draw a piano at the centre to keep you focused.

2. Bearing in mind your associations, and the description of the piano being dug out and reassembled by the community after the tsunami, write a paragraph giving your thoughts on what the piano symbolises (what it stands for or represents) in the poem.

3. What is the effect of key words and phrases in the poem? Copy and complete the table below to explore this. Add at least two more words or phrases.

Quotation	Effect
'writhe and groan'	Personifies the piano, as if it is a person in great pain, reflecting the suffering of the people because of the tsunami.
'scattered'	Makes it sound random, as if …
'lamented'	

NOW TRY THIS

1 Write an upbeat, heart-warming local newspaper feature about the renovation of the piano. Remember to include:

- ✪ what happened
- ✪ how it happened
- ✪ when and where it happened
- ✪ who was involved
- ✪ why it is important to the community
- ✪ what will happen to the piano now.

2 Think of some other significant object that might have been discovered in the mud and mended after the tsunami. Compose a poem or piece of creative writing describing this process.

3 Write an advert appealing to local people for help in restoring a piano or other significant object that was found in the mud. Remember to say how the advertiser can be contacted. It could be headed:

HELP WANTED!

FAST FINISHERS

Write a short speech of thanks that could be made by the local mayor to those involved in the restoration of the piano. Include a comment on why it is important for the community and even for Japan as a whole.

4 In groups of three or four, role-play a TV news piece in which a presenter interviews two or three people who were involved in different ways in discovering and restoring the piano. Aim to give each interviewee a different role. For example, they could be:

- ✪ the person who found the piano sticking out of the mud
- ✪ a local volunteer
- ✪ a piano expert or musician.

Finish with the presenter saying what will happen to the piano now, and thanking the interviewees.

❓ PRACTICE QUESTION

Explore how the poet has used narrative to reveal the story of the piano's restoration and show why it is significant. You could comment on:

- ✪ structure
- ✪ choice of details
- ✪ word choices and their effect
- ✪ the purpose and overall effect of the poem.   [8 marks]

24 Oh, How I Wish To Have A Full-Blooming Cherry Tree

by Junko Kimura, self-translated

LEARNING OBJECTIVES

- To explore language techniques
- To understand the writer's use of symbolism
- To see how texts fit into their cultural and historical settings

CONTEXT

The poem was inspired by the tsunami (a huge wave) that led to a nuclear accident and flooded Fukushima, in Japan, on 11 March 2011. For further context, see page 58.

Somewhat appropriately, the poet's first name, Junko, means 'Born in the Spring'. The poet was born in Hokkaido in 1936.

In Japanese culture, cherry blossom symbolises spring and renewal, but also the briefness of human life – because the blossom lasts only for a short time. The nuclear accident and tsunami occurred just before the start of the blossom season, preventing many cherry trees from blooming.

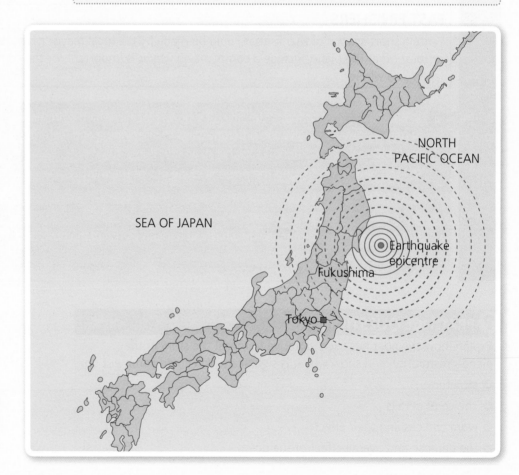

▶ The location of Fukushima in Japan and the regions affected by the 2011 tsunami

Oh, how I wish to have a full-blooming cherry tree
here, in the centre of
this icebound white plain!

The poet is probably commenting on a snowbound landscape, but it seems to represent the destruction caused by the tsunami.

Beginning of the landscape being personified as hard-hearted.

Its frozen heart stolen
by the faint smell of
full-blooming blossoms,
will the icy field forget its pride,
slowly loosening itself and
melt down?

Personification continues, with pride suggesting emotional coldness.

Subtle simile suggesting love.

When pink petals fall in a breeze
slight as a girl's sigh,
will the plain masked in white
slowly melt away,
its face now flushed,
losing self-control?

The hopeful question is the climax of the personification. The pink blossom would be like a blush caused by emotion.

I wish to have a full-blooming cherry tree!
My numbed heart would be at ease
covered by swirls of falling petals.

Neither with radioactive snow,
nor with atomic black rain,
but only with profusely falling petals
will the sky warm the earth.
Only with a rain of pink petals
will the split and severed earth be healed.

Referring to nuclear contamination of water, and to falling radioactive material.

Seems to refer to the earthquake.

Linking the heavens and the earth –

Oh, how I wish to have a full-blooming cherry tree
in the centre of this icy white plain!

The poem ends as it begins, with longing for renewal, but it also gives a sense of completion.

SKILLS FOCUS

✔ Understand the use of symbolism.
✔ Explore language techniques and choices.

LOOK CLOSER

1. The poem is very visual. Describe what mental pictures it makes you see and what ideas or feelings they suggest to you.

2. Explain how the poet uses personification. Consider:
   - what the blossom represents
   - what feeling the poet says the land has
   - what he hopes will happen to the land.

3. What is the effect of key words and phrases in the poem? Copy and complete the table below, and add at least one more quotation.

Quotation	Effect
'full-blooming'	Suggests nature's generosity, and something full of life.
'icebound white plain'	Suggests that the landscape is in the emotionally cold grips of ...
'slight as a girl's sigh'	

NOW TRY THIS

1 Think of a tree you know – either a type of tree (for example, oak, beech, birch) or an actual tree. On a sheet of plain paper, draw a small picture of the tree in the centre of a mind map or spidergram. Then add words or phrases around the image to suggest all the things you might associate with this tree. Here is the beginning of an example:

2 Use your words and phrases to write a poem in which you make the tree, or something about the tree, a symbol. For example, an oak tree could stand for the idea that important things can grow from small ideas, as in the saying, 'Big trees from little acorns grow.'

Here are some other possible associations:

❂ pine/fir tree – Christmas, winter

❂ birch – white, peeling bark, looks ghostly

❂ willow – grows by water, often described as 'weeping'

❂ holly – Christmas, evergreen (thus everlasting life); also prickly, like an unfriendly person?

rough

strength

deep roots

acorns

FAST FINISHERS

Write what a tree might say to you about itself if it could speak. For example, it could comment on:

❂ its deep roots

❂ creatures that live in and on it

❂ its leaves

❂ how it withstands weather, especially storms.

3 Discuss ways in which trees have been important throughout history, and in modern times. For example, you could talk about:

❂ forests as wild places where people could hide – like Robin Hood

❂ forests as habitats for animals – and therefore places to hunt

❂ trees as symbols – for example, the Tree of Knowledge in the Garden of Eden

❂ wood as a material for buildings, furniture, carving, fuel, etc.

❂ the importance of forests like the Amazon as the 'lungs of the planet'.

? PRACTICE QUESTION

How does the poet express hope for the future in 'Oh, How I Wish To Have A Full-Blooming Cherry Tree'? Use examples from the poem as evidence. Consider:

❂ what the cherry blossom means in Japan

❂ symbolism and personification

❂ what you know about the context

❂ language techniques and word choice.

[8 marks]

Key terms

Active verb	When the person or thing does something, rather than has an action done to them.
Adjective	A word that describes a noun; e.g. 'the reckless man'.
Adverb	A word that describes a verb; e.g. 'he ran awkwardly'.
Alliteration	When two or more words begin with the same letter or sound; e.g. 'Jolly giant giraffes jest joyfully in June'.
Analyse	Identify the parts of a topic and explore their links.
Anaphora	When a word or phrase is repeated at the beginning of consecutive lines of writing. It is most commonly used in poems and speeches.
Anecdote	A story from the writer's own personal experience.
Argue	Put the case for or against a view.
Bildungsroman	A story told from a young character's point of view which charts their development as they change and grow.
Colloquial language	Ordinary language used in casual conversation that is not in a formal style.
Compare	To find similar qualities between ideas.
Context	Background information about the writer or the time the text is set.
Contrast	To find different qualities between ideas.
Dialogue	A conversation between two or more people.
Discuss	Consider different views on an issue or argument.
Dramatic irony	When the significance of a character's words or actions is clear to the audience but unknown to a character.
Ellipsis	A set of dots that usually indicates a pause or that words have been intentionally missed out. (Note: the plural is 'ellipses'.)
Emotive language	Language that appeals to a reader's emotions.
End rhyme	Rhyme between a poem's line endings.
Enjambement	In poetry, when a sentence continues from one line to the next line without a pause.
Epithet	An adjective expressing a quality that is typical of the person or thing being described.
Evaluate	Make judgements based on evidence.
Examine	Investigate closely.
Explain	Give reasons for something.
Explicit information	Information that is stated clearly.
Figurative language	Language such as similes, metaphors or personification.
Foreshadowing	When later events in a story are hinted at before they happen.
Identify	Name or set out key features.
Imagery	The use of language to create word pictures by comparing one thing with another; *see also* metaphor, personification, simile.
Imperative	A command or request.
Implicit information	Information that is implied, rather than stated clearly.
Internal rhyme	Rhyme that occurs within a single line of a poem.
Juxtaposition	Putting two contrasting ideas next to each other.
Metaphor	When a word or phrase is used to describe something else; e.g. 'She was on fire', to suggest that she is very good at what she is doing.
Mood	The atmosphere of a piece of writing; e.g. 'scary', 'peaceful', 'exciting', 'dull', 'sad'.
Narrative approach	First person ('I walked'), second person ('You walked') or third person ('He/She/ They walked').
Noun	An object, e.g. 'chair', name, e.g. 'Sarah', or emotion, e.g. 'love'.
Onomatopoeia	When a word sounds like the sound it describes; e.g. 'Bang!'
Paraphrase	Expressing the meaning of something by using different words.
Pathetic fallacy	Where the weather (or other inanimate object) reflects what is happening in a story.
Personification	Describing something that isn't human by using human qualities; e.g. 'The tree danced in the wind'.
Present participle	Ending in '-ing'; e.g. 'I'm thinking'.
Pronoun	A word used in place of a noun or someone's name; e.g. 'I', 'you', 'she', 'they', 'my', 'our', 'themselves'.
Protagonist	One of the major characters in a story.
Quotation	Taking a group of words from a text or speech.
Repetition	Repeating a word or phrase to make it memorable.
Rhetorical question	A question in writing or speech that is used to involve the reader but does not require an answer.
Sibilance	The repetition of 's' sounds for effect; e.g. 'The sly and sinister snake'.
Simile	When something is compared to something else using the words 'like' or 'as'; e.g. 'As snug as a bug', 'cold like ice'.
Summarise	Present the main points and ideas.
Tone	The attitude of a writer towards the subject or his audience; e.g. 'funny', 'sad', 'formal', 'informal', 'sarcastic'.
Verb	An action word; e.g. 'running', 'walked', 'dances'.